HOW TO MAKE AN AMISH QUILT

HOW TO MAKE AN AMISH QUILT

More than 80 beautiful patterns from the quilting heartland of America

Rachel and Kenneth Pellman

Pattern illustrations by Craig N. Heisey

Rodale Press, Emmaus, Pennsylvania

in cooperation with **Good** **Books**® Intercourse, PA 17534

Acknowledgments

Cover Design by Cheryl Benner
Design by Craig N. Heisey and Dawn J. Ranck

We wish to thank Good Books, Intercourse, Pennsylvania, for the preparation of this book. We also wish to thank Good Books for special permission to incorporate large portions of the following books into this special edition: *The World of Amish Quilts* (© 1984), *Amish Quilt Patterns* (© 1984), and *Small Amish Quilt Patterns* (© 1985). All permissions, acknowledgments, and credits for the above mentioned portions hereby apply.

Printed in the United States of America on acid-free paper

If you have any questions or comments concerning this book, please write:
Rodale Press
Book Reader Service
33 East Minor Street
Emmaus, PA 18098

Library of Congress Cataloging-in-Publication Data

Pellman, Rachel T. (Rachel Thomas)
    How to make an Amish quilt: more than 80 beautiful patterns from the quilting heartland of America/Rachel and Kenneth Pellman.
        p. cm.
    Includes index.
    ISBN 0-87857-864-1   hardcover
    1. Quilting—Patterns.   2. Quilts, Amish.   I. Pellman, Kenneth, 1952-
II. Title.
TT835.P444 1989
746.9'7041—dc20   89-33630
                                             CIP

4 6 8 10 9 7 5   hardcover

Table of Contents

Prologue

The World of Amish Quilts

How can the splash of color, synonymous with many Amish quilts, well up from a people whose life is so reserved and disciplined? Is it not both a visual and theological irony for the "quiet-in-the-land" to mix such austerity and beauty?

An encounter with antique Amish quilts is incomplete if it does not include some understanding of the people who made them. If one studies Amish quilts without relating the finished textile to the community of its origin, one is left with only a partial look at these wonderful bedcovers.

The Amish are traditionally recognized for their strict lifestyle. Black hats, drab carriages and sad faces are quick labels often used to identify them. But by wearing the right kind of glasses—those that look beyond oversimplification—one will discover that the Amish live in a delightful world of faith, community and beauty.

Beauty and craftsmanship are traditions among the Amish. Meticulously manicured lawns and gardens, correctly shocked stalks of field corn, well groomed houses and barns belong to their way of life. They find joy in the push of a bean through the springtime soil, in filled chairs around the supper table, and Sunday visits. Loaded canning shelves and full hay mows satisfy their bodies and spirits. To do something well and attractively is always more gratifying for them than doing one of those qualities without the other.

Who Are These People?

Who are these people? Where did they come from? Where are they going? Why do they live the way they do?

The Amish are, most basically, a people committed to God. They believe that their lifestyle and practice must embody their faith. They intend to live, in every part of life, consistently with Jesus' teachings in the New Testament.

The Amish believe that Jesus taught his followers to be a community to each other that nurtures its members to

greater faithfulness. It is from this unique belief that the Amish receive much of the solidarity they need to continue living with the tensions they feel with the outside world. One cannot be Amish alone. It requires the support and fellowship of others who share the same beliefs. The community becomes the conscience for the individual. And the community discerns together the do's and don'ts for its members.

Community is a Refuge

Most Amish do not see their community as restrictive. Rather, it is a harbor from rampant Western individualism they believe responsible for the demise of the church, home and family. It is against this backdrop that the Amish church continues to grow, having doubled in size in the last twenty years. There is peace, security and joy in living as the Amish do. Though not without its struggles and problems, the Amish community nurtures its members in wonderful and precious ways.

So as a result of trying to follow their faith daily in life the Amish find themselves to be separate from the world. And because they are committed to their faith-life, they are wary of anything that could become a possible route to acculturation into the "world." The Amish believe that becoming involved in the larger society takes one away from family, community and church. Their leaders are constantly concerned with the purity of their fellowship. So they tend to draw lines in black and white areas before the issues become gray to help identify their church's separation from the world.

The Old Order Amish (the strictest of all the Amish groups) have traditionally shunned the use of electricity from local power companies, have not permitted telephones in their homes, have rejected ownership of automobiles and usually discontinue their formal education on the completion of grade eight. Their farming is generally

How To Make an Amish Quilt

How To Make an Amish Quilt

done with horses and mules. Dress regulations are quite severe. Solid colored fabrics are usually the rule for men's and women's clothing. Their primary language within the community is Pennsylvania Dutch (Deutsch) although they are also fluent in English. Yet the Amish are not simply figures cut from the very same form. They are individuals, and as a result, diverse within the structures. It is this blend of diversity and regulation that keeps the Amish culture alive and vital.

The Problem with Technology

For the Amish, advanced technology is not evil or wicked in itself. They do not think that a vehicle with four wheels that travels at high rates of speed is necessarily designed by ungodly forces. But the Amish do believe that the automobile is a major factor in breaking up the family. A car in the driveway increases the temptation to be places other than home, thus making it difficult to spend the majority of evenings each week with one's family.

The same concern is behind the Amish rejection of electricity from local power companies. The Amish are not opposed to the correct alignment of electrons and neutrons that produces electricity. Their caution is that if it is too readily available in the house, members could be tempted to acquire all kinds of appliances and gadgets that may lead to the accumulation of possessions and luxury. They may buy a radio. And if a radio, why not a television? And if one has a television, why not watch movies that are aired?

And if one watches movies at home, why not go to the theatre and cinema as well? They believe the drift into the world can be subtle. That explains why the Amish are so leery of keeping up with style and technology. Separation from the world, they believe, is a biblical value that also holds them together as a people of god.

While these generalizations are true for most of the Amish groups spread throughout many states, there are always exceptions. Blanket statements can result in an unfair depiction of a people who have individual characters and personalities. So how did these people begin? Where are their religious moorings?

Not a Fly-by-Night Group

The Amish find their roots in the Protestant Reformation. They are a Christian group whose origins are with the reformers who believed that the break Martin Luther and Ulrich Zwingli were making from the state church was neither as extensive or severe as it should be. At that time in the 1500s, the word "Amish" was not used.

The leaders of this radical left wing of the Protestant Reformation believed in a separation of church and state. One could live peaceably within the boundaries of the state but only with the keen understanding that one's first allegiance was to God. If the requests of the state ever conflicted with the group's understanding of Christ and his teachings, the state would have to take a back seat.

There is a serenity about the Amish way. Early morning always brings lots of chores to be done around the farm regardless of the season.

How To Make an Amish Quilt

This small group also practiced adult baptism. They believed baptism to be a symbol of one's commitment to Jesus and the way of life he demonstrated while living on earth. Biblical study showed these reformers that the way of Jesus and the way of the world had difficulty coexisting. Because of potential physical and emotional persecution from people outside their convictions, this group believed one must thoroughly understand these possible hazards before committing oneself to following the values Jesus taught. They believed only adult minds had the capability of making such a tough decision. That is why they performed voluntary baptism for adults. Because of this practice, they were nicknamed by their taunters, "Anabaptists." This title does not mean anti-baptist, but rather re-baptized.

The Anabaptist movement officially began in Zurich, Switzerland on January 21, 1525 when the first group of adults took turns baptizing each other. The beliefs of this group found ready acceptance from many people throughout Europe. The movement flourished, spreading quickly through Germany, France, and the Netherlands. A prolific writer and articulate man from Friesland became known as a prominent leader of the Anabaptists. His name was Menno Simons. It's from his name that people in his church were eventually nicknamed Mennonites.

Church Concerned with Purity

In 1693, a Mennonite minister, Jacob Amman, had a conviction that the church was getting too lax in the enforcement of the discipline that separated them from worldliness. Amman led a difficult and painful split from the Mennonites. The people who followed him were nicknamed Amish.

Because of identical origins and similar faith understandings, the Amish and Mennonites remain much more alike theologically than different. They are like religious cousins. Their differences are primarily evident in their lifestyles and practices rather than in their basic beliefs.

What Distinguishes Antique Amish Quilts?

The quilts in this book are antique Amish quilts. The dates of their origins range from the mid-19th century to the early 20th century. Amish women do continue making quilts today. But these recent quilts look drastically different from the old ones as a result of modern materials and dyes. These contemporary quilts, though made by Amish, are not included in this collection.

Why have many of these antique quilts gained the attention of art critics in the larger world? Why are they in such demand by collectors? Why are they escalating in value as investment objects? There are many answers. It is nearly impossible to acquire the same fabrics and dyes used in antique Amish quilts. Natural fibers dyed at home with

Children are an integral part of the Amish community. Their dress and language reflect who they are expected to become.

natural pigments produced a warm vibrance, unattainable in modern fabrics. There is also an exceptional artistic quality present in these quilts.

Art, for itself, is frowned on within the Amish community. Amish women never formally study color or line in an attempt to design an aesthetically pleasing quilt. That a quilt functions warmly and well as a bedcover was a quiltmaker's primary concern. Because these quilts were not designed to be art objects, they become most interesting if they are not removed from the context in which they were constructed.

An "Innocent" Creativity

Something about the wholeness of life in the Amish community has produced and permitted the mix of superior craftsmanship and visual quality. Creativity has thrived in Amish quilts. The Amish communities' uneducated approach to color has resulted in daring bursts and subtle blends of color. Within the Amish setting little attention is given to color coordinating clothing or home decor. One wears the colors allowed by the church and plants the flowers created by God. It seems to be this freedom from color theory and an uninhibited use of bright colors that has produced some wonderful masterpieces. Not all old Amish quilts, however, fall into this delightful category!

Turgid colors and geometric shapes are typical in the quilts of this disciplined people. Stars created from diamond-shaped pieces of fabric are common among Eastern and Midwestern Amish.

What Inspired These Patterns?

Trying to decide the origin of any given quilt pattern soon becomes mere speculation. But an understanding of the rural agrarian environment that produced these quilt-makers is helpful. Fences around pastures certainly create straight line imagery, depicted in Bars and Rail Fence patterns. Star quilt patterns and the heavenly bodies seem to have a common motif. Fan quilts and buggy wheels may be related. Windmills that pump water and Pinwheel patterns have a similar design. And the parallels between nature and quilt patterns continue. This type of conjecture is difficult to prove. But finding skyscraper, subway or computer motifs in Amish quilts is even more difficult!

Many Amish quilt patterns have specific names but abstract geometric shapes. Realism in pieced quilt tops is not generally permitted by the Amish church. Images are suggested but not definitely constructed. For example, one can see an interlocking log motif in the Log Cabin even though there is no door, roof, or windows. And because of the difficulty of attaching two curved pieces of fabric to each other without puckers, most pieced quilt shapes have straight edges. Squares, rectangles, diamonds and triangles make up the basic group of geometric designs used. The majority of Amish quilts are assembled using these four main shapes.

Putting Quilts Together

Quilt tops are constructed in two primary ways—by piecing and by appliqueing. Piecing means that the top layer of fabrics on a quilt are sewn to each other along common edges. The result is a single layer of fabric with seam allowances on the reverse side. This piecing is usually done with a sewing machine.

Appliquéing is the process of sewing by hand, one piece of fabric to the surface of another, making sure raw edges are hidden. Because a quiltmaker does not want a quilt to have a puckered surface when it is finished, this procedure is more tedious and time-consuming than piecing. Appliqueing is usually done when curved pieces of fabric are required in the pattern under construction. The tiny hidden stitches of skillful appliquéing are achieved only by long-time veteran quilters.

While straight-edged geometric shapes usually make up the pieced top, the lavish quilting that nearly smothers them is often full of curves and circles. Realism is more acceptable in this intricate stitching. Fruit and flower designs are found occasionally in quilting, alongside the more common feather, plant, waffle, and medallion motifs.

Quilting Stitches Are Functional

The elaborate stitchery that envelops these bedcovers is

viewed as functional within the Amish world. A quilt is composed of three layers. And the quilting is needed to hold those three layers together. The top is the pieced or appliquéd surface. This side of the quilt boasts the colors and pattern which gives the quilt its name. Quilts also have backs. This surface rarely has any pieced or appliquéd pattern and is the bottom layer of the quilt. (Frequently the skill of the quilting stitches is more visible on this reversed side because there is no variation of color or pieces to compete with the viewer's attention.) Sandwiched between the top and back is the lining. This middle layer provides warmth, but also serves to enhance the quilting. Because the lining is usually thicker than the top or back, its puffy quality shows off the masterful stitches of Amish quilters.

The word "quilting" is both a noun and a verb. The verb "quilting" is the actual process of hand-stitching the three layers of the quilt together. Great care and attention is given to keeping those small running stitches as tiny and straight as possible. With old fabrics and old linings, a good quilter could line up as many as five stitches on a needle at one time and get two full needles' worth of stitches per inch. The finished stitches are also referred to as "quilting." They anchor the lining between the top and back to keep it from bunching up.

Knotting Comforters

Another method of attaching the layers of a quilt together is by knotting. This process is much less tedious and time-consuming. One stitch with a heavy thread is drawn through all three layers of the quilt and then the two ends of the thread are knotted together on the top. This procedure is done in regular two or three inch intervals. The ends of the thread, which are often a contrasting color, are not clipped closely. Instead the tails are nearly an inch long to be sure the knot does not open. These knotted bed-covers are usually called comforters.

Diversity in Amish Quilts

People often perceive the Amish to be backward and against all change. But is a group who contributes almost nothing to air pollution, for example, really backward? Their home-grown meat and vegetables lack chemical preservatives; crime and divorce are nearly unheard of within their community. But this is not to imply that the Amish are static. They do experience change, but at a less frantic pace than most of their non-Amish neighbors. Their increased use of diesel power, extensive use of pneumatic tools and appliances, and their more frequent riding of bicycles signal change in some of the communities.

Nor has the quilting world of the Amish been exempt from change either. Pattern types and variations, the size of pieces, and color have all evolved. There are marked geographical and chronological differences visible in Amish quilts. The eastern settlements are older than those in the West, so Amish quilts from Pennsylvania can be traced to an earlier period than those from Ohio or Indiana. It also appears fair to suggest that there was greater wealth among the Lancaster County Amish than those in the Midwest. It seems likely that many Lancaster County women bought fabric for the express purpose of making quilts. Center Diamond patterns, for instance, require larger pieces of fabric than would be left as scraps from making clothing. The Pennsylvania communities were more economically stable than were the newer communities settling in the Midwest. The financial instability that came from moving to new areas was reflected in the more common use of clothing scraps in the quilts made by midwestern women. Frugality, as well as the limited accessibility of fabric stores, also accounts for the popularity of certain quilt patterns. Along with smaller pieces, midwestern quilts also boasted more lively colors.

This funeral procession depicts the support of the community for its members even in death. These buggies have just left the funeral service held at the home of the deceased, and are on their way to a family grave plot where the body will be laid to rest.

More Borrowing in the Midwest

The distances between midwestern Amish settlements were greater than in Pennsylvania. So the Amish visited less with each other and had greater interaction with their "English" (the Amish term for people who are not in their church) neighbors. With that increased outside influence, the midwestern Amish adopted more daring patterns, borrowing some from neighbors and reworking old standard patterns. Consequently there is a broader spread of patterns and colors from these more farflung communities than from the more densely populated eastern settlements. But no matter their geographic origin, antique Amish quilts possess an energy that is rooted in a complex milieu of diversity and conformity, of restriction and freedom.

Introduction

The magic of Amish quilts has begun to capture admirers everywhere. Perhaps it is the simplicity and peace visible in the lives of the people who create them that has made these quilts so fascinating. Perhaps it is the combination of energy and restraint in these quilts' simple geometric patterns that gives them such broad appeal. Perhaps in a modern, fast-moving technological age, people grasp for links with the past to find stability. Whatever the impetus, there is increasing interest in Amish quilts.

From Simple Quilts to Collectors' Items

This growing demand for Amish quilts has been felt deeply throughout Amish communities. It began with old quilts from the larger Amish settlements of eastern Pennsylvania and the Midwest being purchased from private homes by museums and collectors. As the quilts gained more attention, the Amish communities were ravaged by "door knockers"—people who stopped randomly at Amish homes offering to buy any old quilts. Some old quilts were stolen from homes while the family was away at church. That sort of brazen thievery understandably made the Amish community uneasy, so some owners decided to sell their quilts before they were stolen. Some wanted to sell but wished to wait until the market drove the prices higher. Others wanted to keep their quilts and got weary of questions. But most did not understand the unusual demand.

Within the Amish community, values and commitments are taught and passed on to the next generations through a way of life. Consequently, for the Amish, a tangible symbol of their past is not important or sought after because their basic values are firm and generally not losing ground. And so, many old quilts left homes with their sellers happy to have the cash instead.

For those outside the Amish community, these old quilts stand as symbols of the past. They speak of a time of long evenings spent among family, of winter leisure and handcrafted works of love. Their bold shapes and dark, vibrant colors show stability and freedom within specific limitations.

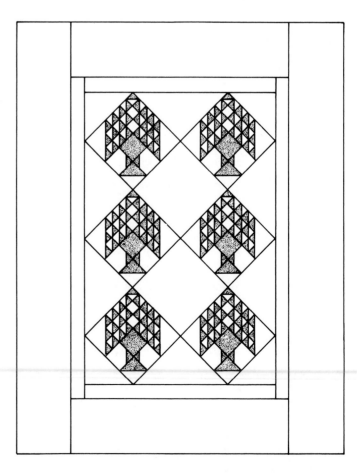

How To Make an Amish Quilt

Creating Your Own Amish Quilt

Many people continue to search for these works of art from the past. But antique quilts are increasingly hard to find. *How to Make an Amish Quilt* allows you to have the next best thing—a good reproduction. Strikingly true reproductions have been made by using old fabrics. But it is also possible to come close to the old look with careful attention to fabric selection, pattern, scale, and quilting designs. This book provides those patterns in the proper scale and with easy-to-follow instructions so that anyone can make one of these prized quilts.

We have enlarged the patterns in their proper proportions to accommodate today's bed sizes. Patterns have also been reduced in size so that the proportions will be pleasing in a small quilt. Templates for piecing, as well as quilting designs, are given in actual size so that there's no need to spend time enlarging. Though they are suitable for bed quilts, these patterns should not be limited to that. They make dynamic wallhangings and can be custom-designed to suit both your color and space requirements.

When used as wallhangings, these quilts are striking display pieces and can be painstakingly pieced and quilted without the fear of wear and tear caused by normal use. On the other hand, what better gift can be given than a handmade quilt to cuddle and comfort a loved one through the dark night hours!

Getting Started

Good planning is the most basic rule in successful quiltmaking. It will minimize many frustrations! A beginning quilter will find it easier to work with a pattern that can be assembled in straight line units, rather than one that requires setting in triangles. For example, the Nine Patch pattern can be done in a series of straight lines, whereas the Lone Star quilt requires setting a triangular-shaped piece into a corner. Study the assembly instructions of a pattern and choose one that provides an adequate challenge without undue difficulty.

You should know before selecting your fabric which quilt pattern you are going to make, how many colors you will need to complete your choice, and which colors or color families you want to use. Since it is difficult to visualize a grouping of colors and fabrics in a quilt when working with either large bolts or small swatches, it is helpful to sketch a scale model of the quilt onto graph paper and then use crayons or colored pencils to fill in the appropriate colors.

Making a Model

You can get an even more accurate color representation by purchasing small amounts of the fabrics under consideration and cutting them into tiny patches to cover the appropriate areas on the scale model. This is especially helpful when working with those patterns using large geometric shapes. This process does become more tedious when working with patterns involving small patches. But the time that goes into making a model is well spent since it allows you to see in advance whether one fabric becomes lost or dominates the others. If, for instance, you are trying to emphasize a particular design within a patch, the surrounding areas will need to provide adequate contrast so that the design pattern will stand out. This dimension can be achieved with light and dark fabrics or by the use of contrasting colors.

Examples of successful contrast can be seen in the Log Cabin quilt on page 57. Light and dark fabrics have been arranged within the individual patches so as to create a barn-raising design on the total quilt. The definition of the T-shapes on the Double T quilt, page 65, can be enhanced or reduced, depending upon the contrast of the fabrics selected for each patch. The bold, bright patches of the Crown of Thorns quilt, page 145, are sharply outlined against the black field. Keep these examples in mind as you choose and arrange the colors in your own quilt.

Choosing Good Fabric

The quality of a quilt is only as good as the quality of each of its components. That is why it is essential to choose high quality fabrics for quiltmaking.

Lightweight 100% cotton or cotton/polyester blends are ideal for quiltmaking. In addition, 100% cottons have a dull finish, making them similar to the fabrics of former days. (Cottons blended with synthetics tend to have more luster or sheen.) The fabric should be tightly woven so it does not ravel excessively. If you check its cut edges and find it frays easily, the fabric will be difficult to work with, especially in small pieces.

Test the fabric for wrinkling by grasping a handful and squeezing firmly. If sharp creases remain when the fabric is released, it will wrinkle as you work with it and will not have a smooth appearance, especially if it is used in large sections on a quilt. It is wise to wash all fabrics before using them to preshrink and test them for colorfastness.

Selecting "Amish" Colors

In the past as well as today, Amish homes are bare by most American standards. Because of their commitment to simplicity, the Amish have traditionally given very little effort to coordinating room decor and accessories. The same is true of their clothing. The Amish style of dress is prescribed by the church. Concern about the latest styles or fashion colors has simply never applied to the Amish way of life. Consequently, the Amish are not bound by the surrounding culture's sense of what is proper and what is not.

This freedom from the dictates of society's norm is evident in the color schemes of antique Amish quilts. When Amish women emptied their scrap bags they didn't work from a basis of color theory. They just chose their fabrics by how well they related to each other. Many times the result was a dramatic color scheme that stands up well today.

It would be unfair to create the impression that all Amish quilts have masterful color combinations. There are many that are less than pleasingly coordinated. But if you would like to capture the best in antique Amish quilt

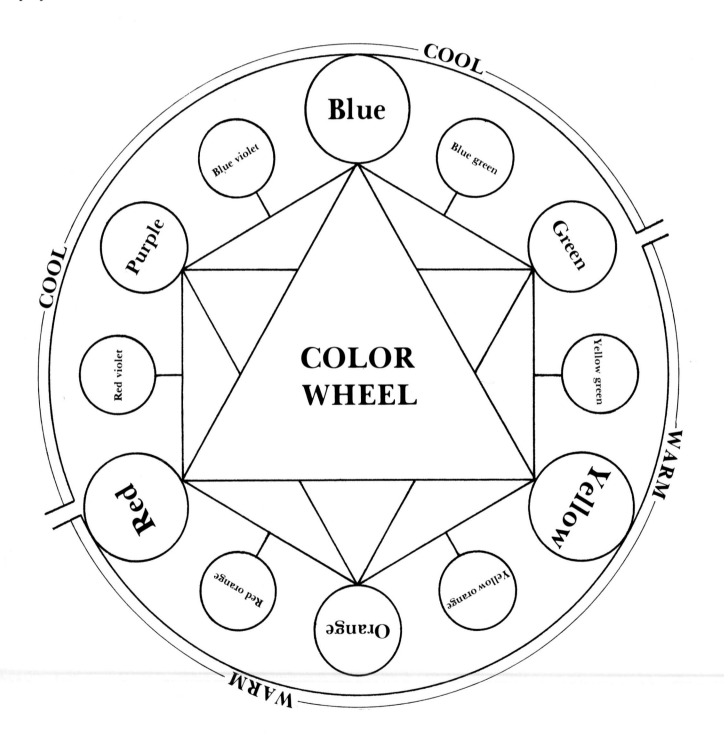

colors, you will be most successful if you try to forget what you know about color and begin with a fresh new approach.

The fabrics used in antique Amish quilts are almost always solid colors. Printed fabrics seldom appear. The oldest, most traditional Amish quilts come from eastern Pennsylvania, specifically from the Amish of Lancaster County. This earliest settlement, historically and today, has tended to be more conservative than some of those which developed later in other areas. For their clothing colors, the Lancaster group used only part of the spectrum of the color wheel, avoiding those colors known as warm colors—bright red, red-orange, orange, yellow-orange, yellow, and yellow-green. Instead, the cool colors—burgundies, blues, purples, and greens—were the colors permitted for clothing and also those used in quilts. These more conservative, traditional Amish quilts did use a myriad of colors, but reflected their community's standards by using only those within the boundaries of that cooler spectrum.

Antique Amish quilts from areas outside the eastern Pennsylvania communities were often more daring in their colors. Yellows and oranges appear frequently in midwestern quilts and those from Pennsylvania counties other than Lancaster. However, these colors are used in conjunction with the traditional darker hues.

Play with colors in several arrangements before you make a final choice for your quilt. See how they stand in reference to each other. Some colors highlight one another and others dull each other. Notice, for example, the combination of colors in the Sunshine and Shadow quilt on page 30. If you look closely, you can see that each color is used in more than one shade. The finished quilt gives the effect of wide bands of graduated color, blending in an easy flow from one to the next.

Try, as much as you can, to approach your color selection in an uninhibited way. The closer you can get to that approach, the more likely it is that you can create a quilt that looks authentically Amish. Look through the quilts pictured in this book, paying special attention to the color choices and noticing which combinations you find effective. Certain combinations are surprising and vibrant; others are subtle and gently modulated.

Don't Forget Black

To approximate Amish color choices, you will do best by using colors of varying intensities and shades. And don't forget black, which may be just the touch you need to add a spark of life to a color scheme. Several shades of black may be even more interesting than only one. The varying shades that appear in old quilts happened because they were often made from scraps, and substitutions were commonly made for fabrics that ran out. You should not be afraid to try substituting one or several similar fabrics instead of using the same one throughout the quilt to create this effect on your own.

Figuring the Yardage

Each pattern in the book provides measurements for all the patchwork pieces and the borders, as well as the dimensions of the finished quilt. Using these measurements you can calculate the necessary yardage for each color used on the front and back and for the borders.

Keep this general rule in mind as you do your calculations: be sure to include the seam allowances (shown on each patchwork piece) when you figure the yardage you will need to buy. The seam allowance (1/4 inch in width) is the lighter black line which outlines each piecing template. The bold black line indicates the actual size of the piece after sewing.

Where templates are *not* drawn, the measurements are given *without* seam allowances. When calculating the amount of fabric needed for those patches, you must add 1/4 inch to each side of each template piece.

It is a good idea to remove all selvages from fabrics before cutting, so allow for that when calculating the width of the fabric you need. Most quilting fabrics are 45 inches wide.

Figure the total yardage you need for patchwork pieces by calculating the amount of fabric needed of each color per block, and then multiply that by the number of blocks in the quilt. (If there will be fabric left from the borders and back, and if you intend to use patches of that fabric, delete that amount from the quantity of that color you are purchasing for patches.)

The border looks best if it does not need to be pieced. Therefore, purchase enough fabric to run the entire length of the quilt. Any fabric remaining along the edges after the borders are cut can be cut into patches for the top.

Since most quilts are wider than 45 inches, you will likely need to piece the back of the quilt. When figuring yardage requirements, remember that the back should be two to three inches larger than the quilt top to make quilting easier. Add that additional fabric into your yardage figures. You should buy enough fabric so that it can run the full length or width without being pieced. Then buy as many lengths or widths as you need to cover the quilt back. Remember to include the seam allowance in your figures.

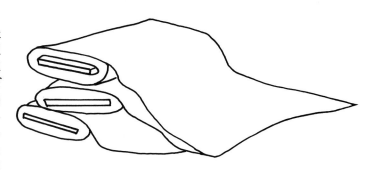

Border Treatments

The border is an important part of a quilt, since it serves as a "frame" that highlights the quilt pattern. Many Amish quilts have wide, elaborately quilted borders. The border on your quilt doesn't have to be fancy, but it should be in proportion to the interior pattern of the quilt. To simplify your quiltmaking, each

long sides and short sides will meet at each corner.

Finally, open the border pieces and with their right sides together, sew the corner seams. The 1/4-inch seam allowance left open at the ends of each border will now be used as the seam allowance on the mitered corner. Stitch from inside corner to outside edge. Backstitch to secure seams at ends (Step 3).

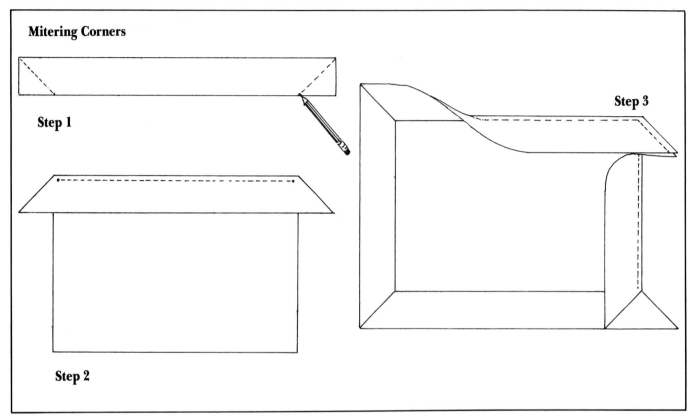

Mitering Corners

Step 1

Step 2

Step 3

quilt pattern in the book provides a suggested border width with instructions for making the border.

One approach preferred by some quilters, although seldom used on antique Amish quilts, is to miter the border of the quilt. To create mitered corners you bring the edges together (on the front of the quilt) at a 45 degree angle in each of the four corners.

To cut borders that will be mitered, start by measuring the length of the quilt top. Add to that figure the border width times 2. For example, if the length of the quilt is 60 inches and the border is 5 inches wide, you will cut the border to be 70 inches, or 60 plus 5 times 2.

On the right side of each border piece, measure in from each end the exact number of inches as the border width. Using a straight edge, draw a diagonal line from that point to the outer corner. Cut along the angled line (Step 1).

With right sides together, stitch the border to the quilt top, leaving the 1/4-inch seam allowance open at each end. Continue with the remaining border pieces, always stopping stitching 1/4 inch from the edge. Be careful not to sew through the already attached border piece(s) (Step 2). If you have sewn correctly, the final stitches on the

Pattern Templates

The accuracy of a template will make a monumental difference in whether a quilt fits together or not. Templates should be very accurately traced onto a material that will withstand repeated outlining without wearing down at the edges. Cardboard is not appropriate for a template that will be used over and over. More durable materials are plastic lids from throw-away containers, the sides of a plastic milk or bleach jug, old linoleum scraps, or tin. (If tin is used beware of sharp edges). Sandpaper may be glued to the back of the template to keep it from slipping as you mark the fabrics.

Before you cut all the quilt's patches, cut enough for just one block by using the new template. Then assemble the pieces in the block to check for accuracy. If changes are required (perhaps the corners don't meet), adjust the template and try again. Always test the template by assembling one block before cutting fabric for an entire quilt top.

Templates may be made with or without a seam allowance, depending on the method of marking, cutting, and piecing preferred by the quilter. The important thing is to maintain accuracy by whatever method is most comfortable for you.

It is extremely critical to be precise in marking and cutting. A minute mistake in either step will be multiplied many times over when you try to assemble the quilt. Ultimately, you want to have a smooth, flat quilt top. To achieve that, the individual pieces must fit precisely together.

Marking Patches with Seam Allowances

To include the seam allowance when marking your patches, draw along the lighter, outside line of the template. That line becomes your cutting line. The seam line is 1/4 inch inside that marked line. The advantage of this method is that if you work with a very sharp scissors, you can trace the outline on the top layer of fabric, then cut through several layers of fabric at the same time. The disadvantage is that when you begin stitching the patches together, you won't have the exact location of the 1/4-inch seam allowance marked directly on the fabric. You must be able to accurately guess the width of the seam allowance so that the corners of the patches meet precisely. Many sewing machines provide marks for different width seam allowances that you can use as a guide as you feed the fabric through.

Marking Patches without Seam Allowances

In this method the template is the actual size of the finished patch. Trace along the darker, inside line (so as *not* to include the seam allowance). That marked line becomes your *stitching* line. The cutting line must be imagined 1/4 inch outside this line. The advantage here is that you have a tracing line to stitch along, almost guaranteeing accuracy in piecing. The disadvantage is that each patch must be marked and cut individually. With this method you cannot stack and cut multiple layers of fabrics.

Tools for Marking and Cutting

There are several ways to mark fabrics. The simplest is to use a regular lead pencil to trace the templates. However, on some fabrics, especially dark fabrics, markings from a lead pencil are very difficult to see. There are several pencils designed especially for quilters. The most popular of these are washable marking pens. When used correctly, the ink disappears without a trace with a little cold water. (These pens are also useful for tracing quilting designs onto the finished front.) Whatever marker you choose, be sure to follow the manufacturer's instructions for its use.

Every quiltmaker should have a good pair of sharp fabric shears. The longer the blade of the scissors, the easier it is to cut a continuous straight line. The scissors must be sharp all the way to the point to cut well-defined corners.

Rotary cutters, consisting of a round blade on a handle, are also readily available in many quilt shops and can be used efficiently in cutting patches. When cutting fabric, the blade and cutting surface should be protected by using a rotary cutting board. Hold the blade against a straight-edge and cut several layers of fabric accurately and quickly.

Piecing

You may piece a quilt either by hand or by machine. Hand-piecing is a more time-consuming and laborious process and most quilters today choose to piece by machine. However, when very small pieces are used and when several points need to meet, hand-piecing is the most precise method. This technique also allows you to work on the project anywhere rather than being tied to the sewing machine. If hand-piecing is used for the blocks, the borders and the sashing between blocks can still be stitched on the sewing machine to save time.

The hand-piecing technique is very simple. You must pin the patches with the right sides together and with their stitching lines perfectly matched. Using a fine sharp needle, make short running stitches through both layers of fabric. The stitches must be straight, even, and tight to achieve an accurate and strong seam. Check stitches periodically to be sure they are not causing puckering. Put an occasional backstitch in with the running stitches to tighten the seam without creating puckers. At the end of the patch, backstitch and knot the thread before clipping. Open the patches and check the seam for precision.

Machine-piecing is obviously a lot faster. The procedure is basically the same as hand-piecing, but the stitching is done by machine. Pin patches together accurately and watch carefully that they do not slip when going through the machine. In machine stitching there are no knots, so it is important to backstitch whenever beginning or ending a seam.

When piecing, whether by hand or by machine, always begin by assembling the smaller patches and build them onto the larger pieces to form the quilt block. Combine patches to form straight sewing lines whenever you can (as an example, see the Assembly Instructions for the Bear Paw Quilt on page 151). You will want to avoid having to set in squares and triangles if at all possible, since stitching around corners requires utmost care to prevent bunching and puckering. When setting in is required, as in star patterns made from diamonds, it is important to stitch the patches that need to be set against each other only to the ends of their stitching lines. And remember not to stitch through their seam allowances.

The seam allowance must be kept free to fit against the seam allowance on the piece being added.

There are two ways to set in a corner. One is to start at the outer edge of one patch, stitch its full length (stopping at the seam allowance), pivot and proceed along the other edge. The other method is to begin stitching along the edge at the center or inner corner. Stitch from the inner corner to one outside edge, backstitch and cut the thread, and then go back to the corner and stitch the remaining edge. Practice both methods and use the one that's easiest for you.

When joining units of patches to each other there is always the problem of what to do with the seam allowances. Seam allowances can be troublesome in two situations. If quilting needs to be done through the seam allowances, making small stitches through multiple layers of fabric becomes virtually impossible. And in the second situation, when a seam allowance of a dark fabric is underneath a lighter fabric, it can show through. It is generally a good idea to lay all seam allowances in the same direction. However, if this will create either of the above problems, make an exception and lay the seam allowance the opposite way.

Preferences vary as to whether seams should be pressed or not when piecing a quilt. Some people like a flat pressed surface and feel it contributes to accuracy. Others view pressing seams as an unnecessary step.

Choosing a Batting

The type of batting or lining used in a quilt will affect its finished look. Much of the batting available today is polyester and has a much puffier quality than the linings used in antique quilts. Cotton batting, which is thinner than the polyester kind, is available from some quilt supply shops. Another option is to use a thin sheet blanket or something similar which adds weight and insulation value but retains the flat appearance of the old quilts. These thinner materials also make it easier to have close, even quilting stitches. To insure that the batting will extend to the edges of the quilt, it should be approximately 2 inches larger than the quilt top on all sides. Excess batting and backing should be trimmed even with the quilt top after quilting is completed.

Preparing to Quilt

Quilting is both an action word and a descriptive word. To quilt means the process of stitching three layers of material together to form a heavier whole. The finished stitches, often done in decorative patterns, are called quilting.

A quilt is a sandwich of three layers: the quilt back, the batting or lining which adds insulation, and the top, which is often pieced or appliqued. The three layers are held together by the quilting stitches.

Much of the charm of old Amish quilts comes from

their quilting. These quilts are lavished with quilting designs, leaving few open spaces. This tiny, intricate quilting is essential in reproducing the look of an old quilt. To make it easy for you to add this beautiful detailing, full-size quilting templates are included in this book. Since templates are used repeatedly it is wise to make them of a material more durable than paper. Cardboard or thin plastic are good choices.

Marking designs on the quilt top can be done in a variety of ways. Remember to mark with something that will not rub off easily, because as you are quilting your hands will brush against the surface. But, while you want the markings to last while you are quilting, they should also be completely removable when the quilting is finished so that unsightly lines do not remain.

If you work with fabric that is light enough to see through, the easiest way to mark is by tracing. Outline the quilting designs on paper with a heavy Magic Marker. Lay the fabric to be marked, wrong side down, on top of the quilting design. Trace, with a washable fabric marker, over the lines to be stitched.

Although this method is easiest, many fabrics used in these quilts are too dark to allow lines to show through. Therefore, the design must be traced in an alternate way. This can be done by cutting very thin slashes at close intervals along the lines on the quilting template. These slashes will be used to create a dot-to-dot effect on the fabric. Lay the template on top of the right side of the fabric and poke through the slashes with a fabric marker. (Good markers for dark fabrics include yellow colored pencils, a soapstone marker, or even a skinny piece of handsoap worn to a point on one edge.)

Straight lines or crosshatching can be marked by laying a ruler on the fabric and tracing along both sides. On large areas, a chalk line can be snapped across the quilt to mark the lines accurately and easily. When patches are being outlined by quilting, no marking around them is necessary. Simply quilt close to the seam to emphasize the patch.

Needles and Thread

Quilting is a simple running stitch, most easily done with special quilting thread. This thread is heavier than regular thread and more able to withstand the repeated pulling through the three quilt layers.

Quilting needles are called "betweens." These needles are shorter than "sharps," which are considered the normal handsewing needles. Betweens come in various sizes, which are identified by numbers. Most quilters use a size 7 or 8, although some people prefer the even smaller size 9 needle. (Short needles can give you more control.) The best way to choose a needle size is to try several and then use the one that seems most comfortable. A thimble is a must for quilting since the needles must be pushed repeatedly through three fabric layers. The thimble should fit snugly on the middle finger of the hand used for pushing the quilting needle.

Making Tiny, Even Stitches

To begin quilting, cut a piece of quilting thread about 1 yard in length. Thread the needle and make a single knot at the end of the piece. Entering through the right side, insert the needle through only the quilt top, about 1 inch from where quilting will begin. Bring the needle up at the quilting line and pull the thread through to the knot. Gently tug on the knot until it slips through the fabric and is lodged invisibly underneath the top. This will secure the quilting thread at the beginning. With one hand underneath the quilt and the other on top, push the needle down through all three layers until the hand underneath feels a prick. That indicates that you've been successful and stitched through all the thicknesses! (Experienced quilters develop callouses from this repeated pricking!)

Then with the thimble on your upper hand, tilt the needle upward. Use your lower hand to push up slightly from underneath. As soon as the needle point appears again on top, reinsert it through the layers again. Continue this process until three to five stitches are stacked on the needle. Finally, pull the needle and thread through the fabric to create the quilting pattern. The stitches should be snug but not so tight as to create puckering. Continue the process of stacking stitches onto the needle until the thread runs out. When the length of thread is nearly gone, do a tiny backstitch to secure the thread. Insert the needle again through only the top layer and make a stitch the length of the needle, away from the quilting design. Pull the needle through the surface and snip the thread with the long stitch left buried underneath the quilt top. (The long tail of thread prevents the backstitch from being pulled out.) Thread the needle and begin again.

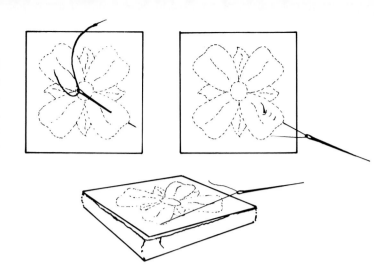

To secure the knot invisibly, insert the needle through the top of the quilt, about 1 inch from where quilting will start. Tug on the knot until it slips through the fabric and is hidden underneath.

The goal to strive for is tiny, even stitches. And they come only with practice! Initially, concentrate on making straight, even stitches, without worrying too much about their size. Try to have the stitch length be the same on both the top and bottom of the quilt. Holding the needle straight is crucial for achieving straight stitches. Then after you have mastered evenness, try to decrease the size of the stitches. When quilting curved lines, do not try to stack a lot of stitches on the needle before pulling it through. No more than two stitches on the needle at a time are best for executing smooth, even curves.

Putting the Quilt in the Frame

In order to achieve a smooth, even quilting surface, it is necessary to stretch all three layers of the quilt in a frame. This creates a taut surface conducive to quilting. The most traditional and probably most effective frame is the type that is large enough to stretch out the entire quilt at one time. This allows for even tension over the whole quilt. These frames are generally used at quiltings when several people work on the quilt at the same time. The disadvantages of such a frame are its size and lack of mobility. Since the entire quilt surface is exposed, the frame obviously requires that much floor space. Also, once the quilt is stretched in the frame it should not be removed until quilting is completed. That usually means that the space is occupied for an extended period of time. Many quilters do not have the space required for such a frame.

Another type of frame accommodates the entire quilt at once, but most of it is rolled onto a long rail along one side of the frame. Only about a three-foot section, along the width of the quilt, is exposed for quilting at a time. As that area is completed the quilt is rolled onto the oppo-

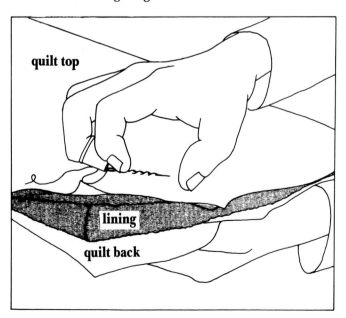

A quilt is a sandwich of three layers — the quilt back, lining or batting, and the quilt top — all held together by the quilting stitches.

site rail, and that sequence is repeated until the entire quilt is finished.

Still smaller frames are available for quilters with very limited space. These look like giant embroidery hoops that allow the quilt to be stitched in small sections. A very important step before using this type of frame is to baste the entire quilt together through all three layers. Begin basting at the center and work out toward the edges. Doing this assures that the layers will be evenly stretched during quilting. It also avoids inadvertently creating puckers during the quilting process. But when you quilt, do not quilt over the basting stitches because this makes them extremely tedious to remove later.

Binding the Quilt

The final step in finishing a quilt is its binding, the strips of fabric that cover the raw edges along the four sides. Bindings, particularly on antique Amish quilts from Pennsylvania, are generally wider than bindings found on many other quilts. And many old Amish quilts use a binding of a color that contrasts with the border and is new to the color scheme of the interior of the quilt.

Since the edge of a quilt receives a lot of wear, the binding is often done with a double thickness of fabric. Bindings can be done in several ways. One of the easier methods is to cut strips of fabric that measure four times the width of the finished binding. These strips can be cut either lengthwise or crosswise on the fabric grain. Piecing on a binding is not very obvious and can be done without minimizing the beauty of the quilt.

The binding strips should measure about one inch longer than the quilt on two of its parallel sides. And on the other two sides, the binding strips should be as long as the quilt's width (or length) plus one inch, plus the finished binding width from the other two sides.

Trim any excess lining and backing from the quilt itself. Fold the binding strips in half, wrong sides together, so that both raw edges meet. Pin the shorter two binding strips against the two parallel edges of the quilt top's width, with the raw edges of the binding flush with the raw edges of the quilt. Machine stitch in place using a 1/4-inch seam allowance. Open the seam so that the folded edge of the binding is now the outer edge of the quilt. Sew the remaining binding strips onto the other sides of the quilt, extending the stitches out to the folded edge of the attached binding strips. Fold the binding in half again so that the previously folded edge goes around to the back and covers the seam made by attaching the strips. Handstitch the binding in place. Fold corners under so that no raw edges are exposed.

Another method of finishing a quilt, less commonly used on old Amish designs, is to simply wrap excess border fabric from the top, bottom, and sides of the quilt around to the back where it is stitched in place. Or the extra backing may be wrapped forward over the raw edges to the front where it is stitched in place on the quilt top.

After the binding is completed, you may want to initial and date the quilt so that it can be identified by future generations. If you sign and date with embroidery, that should probably be done on a lower back corner. Or if you want to quilt in your initials and completion date, that, too, is usually done in a corner.

Displaying Quilts

Wall quilts can be hung in various ways. One is to simply tack the quilt directly to the wall. However, this is potentially damaging to both the quilt and the wall, and unless it is a permanent hanging, it is probably not the best way. Another option is to hang the quilt like a painting. To do so, make a narrow sleeve from matching fabric and hand-sew it to the upper edge of the quilt along the back. Insert a dowel rod through the sleeve and hang the rod by wire or nylon string.

The quilt can also be hung on a frame. This method requires attaching Velcro or fabric to the frame itself. With Velcro, staple one side to the frame. Hand-sew the opposite Velcro onto the edges of the quilt and carefully press these strips onto the Velcro on the frame. Another method for attaching a quilt to a frame is to stitch the quilt to a piece of muslin or another cotton fabric that is 3 inches larger than the quilt on all sides. The fabric can then be stretched gently over a frame, wrapping the excess around the edges to the back and securing them with a staple gun. Quilts can also be mounted inside Plexiglas by a professional framery. This method, often reserved for antique quilts, can provide an acid-free, dirt-free and, with special Plexiglas, a sun-proof environment for your quilt.

Creative Variations on Amish Quilts

All of the quilt patterns in this book come with sizes specified. However, there is still great room for variation. If you want a longer quilt, add a row of patches to the top or bottom. If you need a wider quilt, add patches along each side. Also feel free to vary border treatments. The borders are meant to frame the quilt, and, as long as proper proportions are maintained, they may be pieced in various ways. (For examples of creative border treatments see the Log Cabin quilt, page 57, and the Broken Star quilt, page 70.)

The patches are also adaptable for pillows. A grouping of patches may be used together or a single patch can be enlarged with the use of borders. Pillows can be finished with piping or ruffles, or left plain. Quilt patches can also be used to make pot holders, place mats, table runners and tablecloths, and other craft projects. The only limit is your own imagination.

Total Quilt Assembly Diagram

Quilt projects that follow in the book will refer to these assembly diagrams. Diagrams 1 and 2 are for large-size quilts, and diagrams 3 and 4 are for small-size quilts. Follow the numbers to assemble the pieces in the proper order; the basic sequence is to first assemble blocks in a row before joining rows together.

Diagram 1

Diagram 2

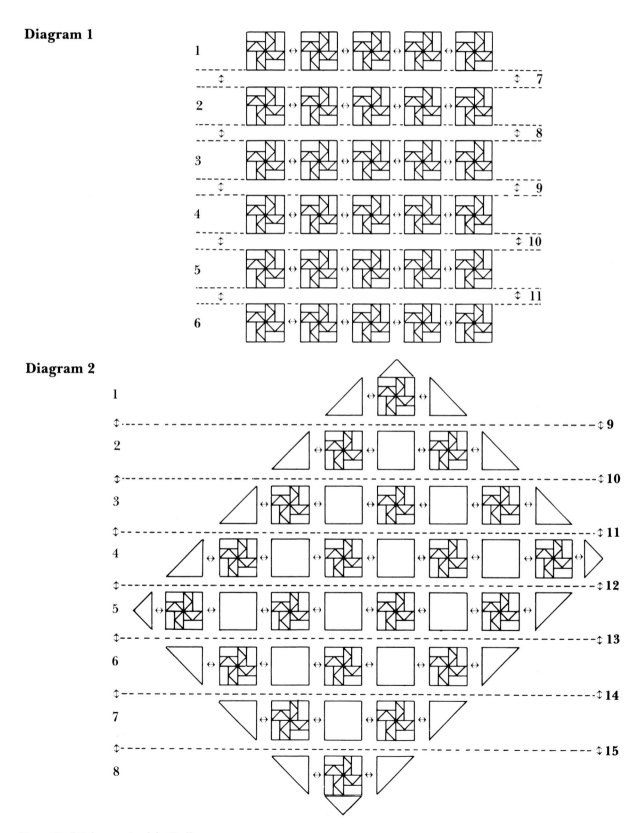

Total Quilt Assembly Diagram

Diagram 3

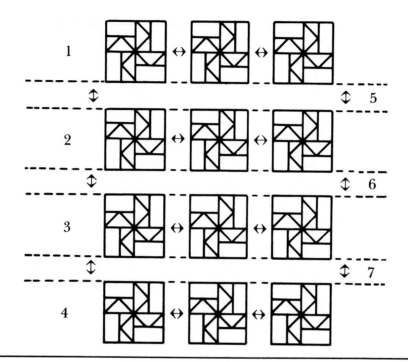

Diagram 4

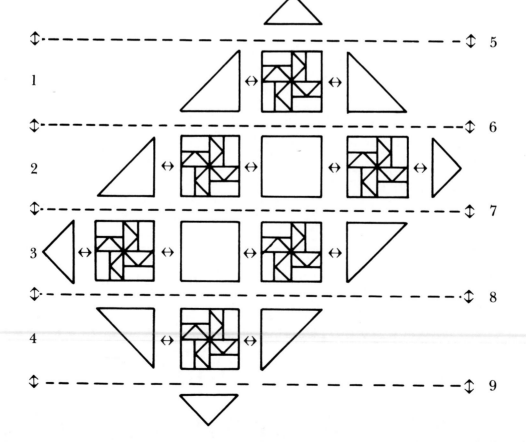

How To Make an Amish Quilt

Border Application Diagram

To obtain correct border length, measure length of edge to which border will be applied. Border widths are given with each pattern. When corner blocks are used, sew them to the ends of the last border pieces and then add the border and blocks as a complete section.

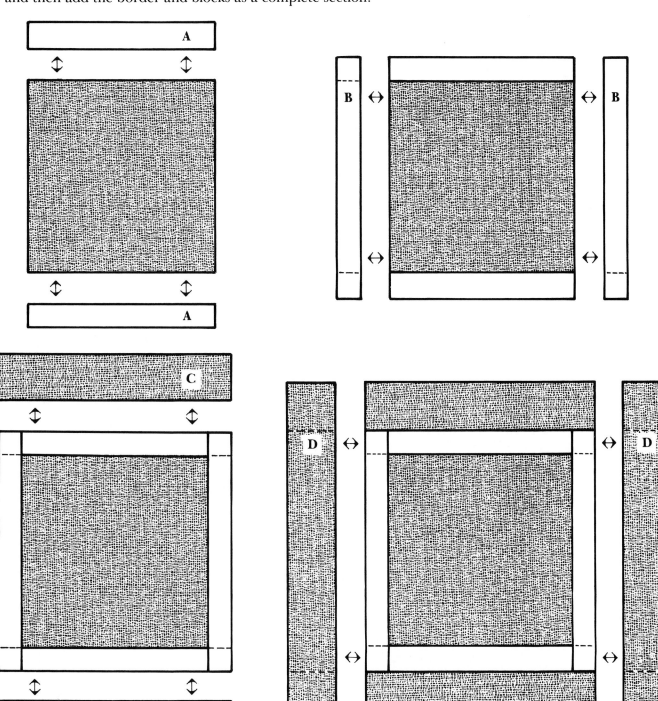

Center Diamond or Diamond in Square

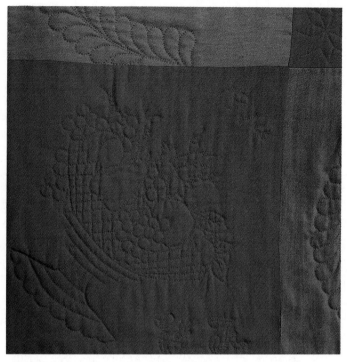

Detail of Center Diamond on facing page.

The suggestion of quilt designs are found all around the farm. Here the standing wheat creates the Diamond in Square, the sheaves the quilting stitches.

The first permanent settlement of Amish in America was in Lancaster County, Pennsylvania. Here, within the strict boundaries of Amish culture, the art of quilting flourished.

One of the oldest and plainest Amish quilt patterns is the Center Diamond, or Diamond in Square, found almost exclusively in Lancaster County quilts. In fact, this design, when discovered in other areas, can often be traced to Lancaster roots.

The pattern is very simple. A large square, made of one central fabric and tipped on its side, forms the diamond. Large triangles fill in the corners to create another square, which is then outlined by one or more borders. Borders may be broken by the addition of corner blocks. The number of colors used may be only two or as many as five.

The fact that such large sections of unbroken fabric are required for this pattern indicates fabrics were likely purchased expressly for use in a particular quilt. By contrast, many other Amish quilt patterns require small patches of fabric and can therefore accommodate scraps left over from other home sewing projects, or salvageable portions of worn-out clothing — a reflection of a frugal lifestyle.

It is difficult to decide what is more outstanding about this quilt — the bold pattern, or the quilting. Center Diamond quilts, with their large open spaces, are usually lavishly quilted with tight, tiny stitches. They are often quilted in dark thread, creating a soft, subtle design on the deep, rich colors of the quilt top surface.

Quilting designs vary, but the central diamond generally has some sort of large, dominant design. Frequently this is a large eight-pointed star inside a feather wreath, or a series of wreaths, the central one filled with small diamonds or cross-hatching. Narrow inner borders, if they are present, may be quilted with rambling grapevines, the pumpkin seed pattern or other narrow designs.

The wide outer borders repeat the generous quilting with elegant curved feathers, ferns, some floral patterns, baskets and other graceful patterns. Corners, especially where blocks are set in, may contain a new and different design rather than continuing the border pattern around the corner.

Although few quilts are signed and dated, careful observation may reveal initials or a date discreetly quilted among the graceful lines of the quilting design.

Center Diamond, dated 1914. Wool, 78 x 77. Lancaster Co., Pennsylvania. The People's Place, Intercourse, Pennsylvania. The date and quilter's initials are beautifully quilted above and beside the overflowing fruit basket in one corner.

Center Diamond
Approximate size 96 x 96

Variation 1

Measurements given <u>without</u> seam allowance

A — 24½ inches square
B — 24½ inches by 6½ inches
C — 6½ inches square
D —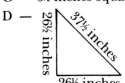

E — 53 inches by 6½ inches
F — 6½ inches square
G — 15 inches by 66 inches
H — 15 inches square

Assembly instructions:

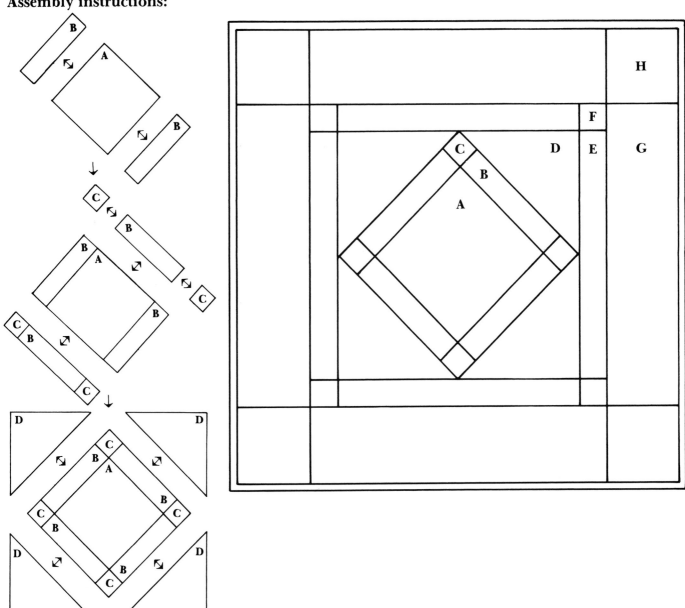

See Border Application Diagram, pg. 23.

Variation 2

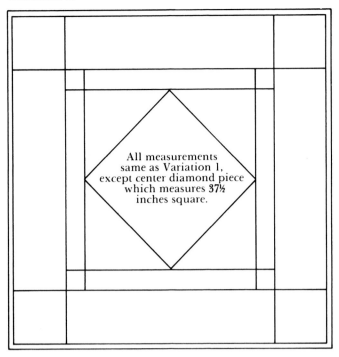

All measurements
same as Variation 1,
except center diamond piece
which measures **37½**
inches square.

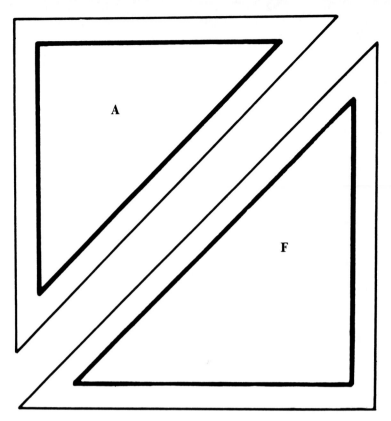

A

F

Variation 3 — Sawtooth Diamond

Measurements given <u>without</u> seam allowance

A — triangle template given
B — 13 1/16 inches square
C — 18¼ inches by 5¼ inches
D — 28¾ inches by 5¼ inches
E —

24 inches / 24 inches / 33 15/16 inches / 24 inches

F — triangle template given
G — 54 inches by 6 inches
H — 66 inches by 6 inches
I — 72 inches by 12 inches
J — 96 inches by 12 inches

Assembly instructions:

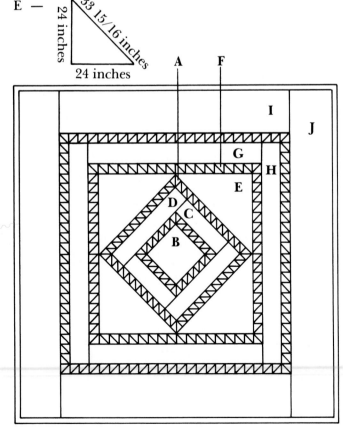

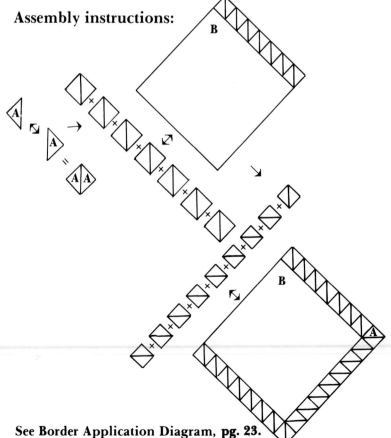

See Border Application Diagram, pg. 23.

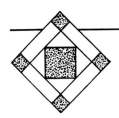

Center Diamond
Approximate size 50 x 50

Variation 1

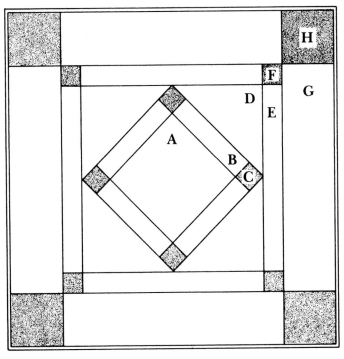

Variation 2

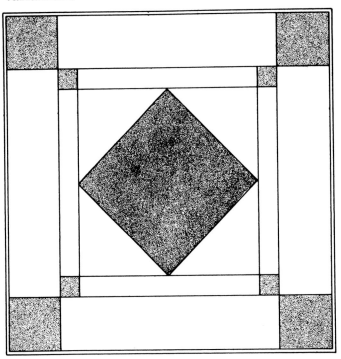

Measurements given <u>without</u> seam allowance

A — 13¾ inches square
B — 13¾ inches by 3 inches
C — 3 inches square
D —

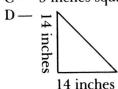

14 inches (vertical), 14 inches (horizontal)

E — 3 inches by 28 inches
F — 3 inches square
G — 8 inches by 34 inches
H — 8 inches square

Variation 2: All measurements are the same except for Center Diamond which measures 19¾ inches square (add seam allowance).

Assembly instructions:

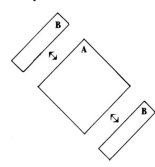 → 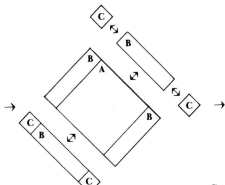 →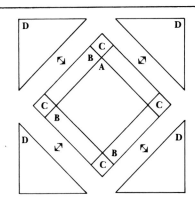

See Border Application Diagram, pg. 23.

How To Make an Amish Quilt

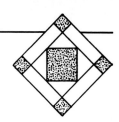

Variation 3—Sawtooth Diamond   Approximate size 48 x 48

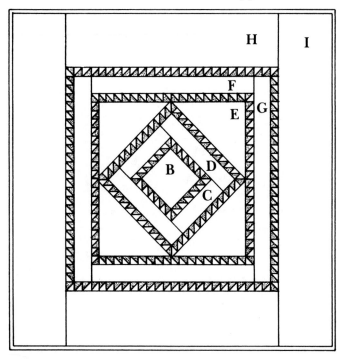

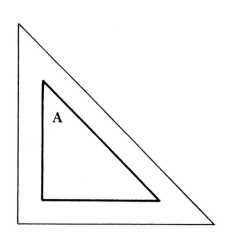

Measurements given <u>without</u> seam allowance

A — triangle template given
B — 6¼ inches square
C — 2½ inches by 8¾ inches
D — 2½ inches by 13¾ inches
E —

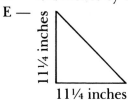

11¼ inches

11¼ inches

F — 2½ inches by 25 inches
G — 2½ inches by 30 inches
H— 8 inches by 32½ inches
I — 8 inches by 48½ inches

Assembly instructions:

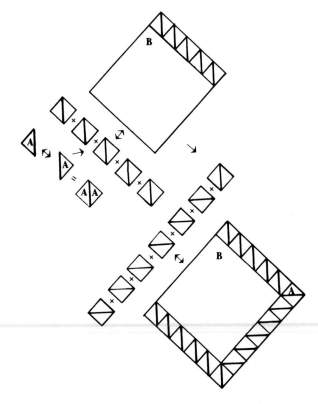

See Border Application Diagram, pg. 23.

Sunshine and Shadow

Sunshine and Shadow, c. 1925-30. Wool, crepe, rayon, cotton, 82 x 84. Lancaster Co., Pennsylvania. William B. Wigton. Effective blending of colors in varying shades in this quilt, which also appears on the cover, add to its drama. Colors are those often used in Amish clothing. A rose motif quilting design fills the border.

Life is full of sunshine and shadows. Death and life exist side by side in the Amish community where birth and old age are equally respected.

There is a striking, almost shocking quality to the Sunshine and Shadow Quilt. Its association with a people of a quiet and subdued lifestyle seems paradoxical. Yet this quilt pattern embodies the spirit of joy and vibrance in the life of an Amish family.

Sunshine and Shadow gets its name from the light and dark effect created by the harmonizing and juxtaposition of a large variety of bold solid colors. The result may be a subtle blending of light to dark or a dramatic opposition of the two.

The Sunshine and Shadow pattern was done largely in Lancaster County, Pennsylvania, but spread to the Midwest when Amish settlements were established there. Therefore, the earliest Sunshine and Shadow quilts are likely Pennsylvania quilts while later ones may be from any Amish area.

This is a simple pattern, consisting of small squares of fabric sewn together and contained by one or several borders. The squares are arranged by color to form a series of brightly colored expanding diamonds. Sometimes the squares are tipped on their sides to form a pattern of squares.

The Sunshine and Shadow quilt traditionally has a wide outer border. Inner borders may or may not be present. Borders may be plain or contain corner blocks.

Because small squares constitute a large part of this quilt, it fits the principle of frugality practiced among the Amish. Most Amish clothes are handmade, often by the women of the household. The scraps left over from these projects could be cut for use in such a quilt. The small pieces required could also come from the still sturdy portions of worn-out clothing.

Quilting on this pattern is lavished on the borders. Here feathers are one of the most common motifs but other full designs are also used. The center squares are often quilted near the seams or simply cross-hatched in diagonal lines. Occasionally a more elaborate stitching like the clamshell design is used on each tiny square. Inner borders usually have their own quilting design the same width as the border itself.

The Sunshine and Shadow arrangement of squares worked with printed fabrics rather than plain, may be called Trip Around the World and is often done by non-Amish women. It is the solid fabrics and the wide borders of the Sunshine and Shadow quilt that make it distinctive and traditionally Amish.

Sunshine and Shadow, c. 1930. Cotton, wool, 81 x 84. Lancaster Co., Pennsylvania. Jay M. and Susen E. Leary. A wide range of colors make this quilt dance.

Sunshine and Shadow
Approximate size 96 x 96

Variation 1

Measurements given <u>without</u> seam allowance

A — square template given
B — 53⅝ inches by 6 3/16 inches
C — 66 inches by 6 3/16 inches
D — 66 inches by 15 inches
E — 15 inches square

Assembly instructions:

$$\boxed{A} + \boxed{A} + \boxed{A} = \boxed{A\ A\ \ \ \ \ } \cdots$$

etc.

See Border Application Diagram, pg. 23.

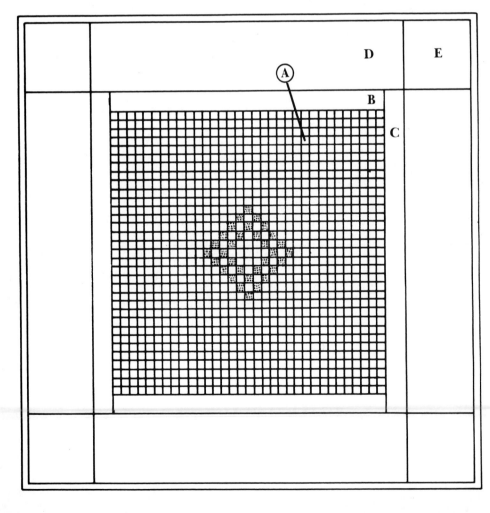

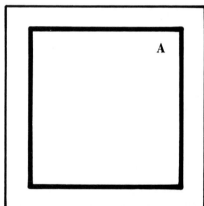

Variation 2 — Center Diamond

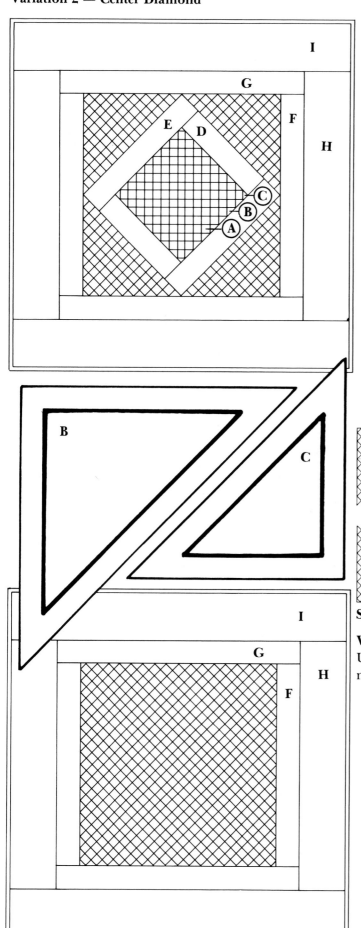

Measurements given <u>without</u> seam allowance

A — square template given
B — triangle template given
C — triangle template given
D — 24 inches by 6 inches
E — 36 inches by 6 inches
F — 51 inches by 6 inches
G — 63 inches by 6 inches
H — 63 inches by 16 inches
I — 95 inches by 16 inches

Assembly instructions:

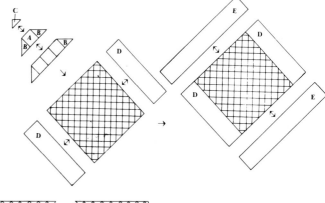

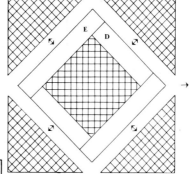

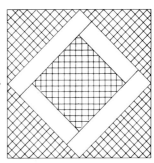

See Border Application Diagram, pg. 23.

Variation 3
Use templates A, B, and C and other indicated measurements from variation 2.

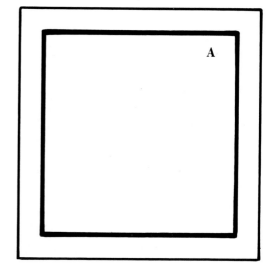

How To Make an Amish Quilt

33

Sunshine and Shadow
Approximate size 50 x 50

Variation 1

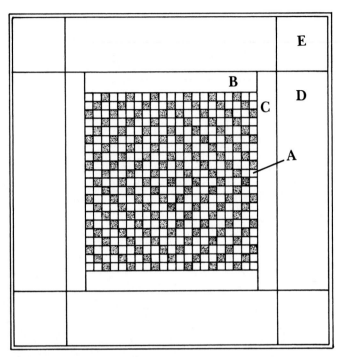

Variation 2—Center Diamond

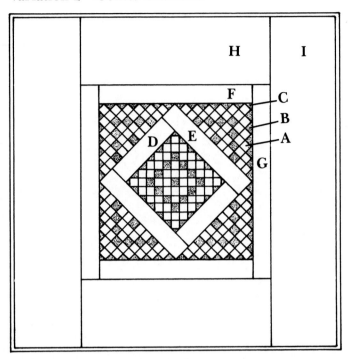

Measurements given <u>without</u> seam allowance

A — square template given
B — 26¼ inches by 3 inches
C — 32¼ inches by 3 inches
D — 32¼ inches by 8 inches
E — 8 inches square

Measurements given <u>without</u> seam allowance

A — square template given
B — triangle template given
C — triangle template given
D — 2¾ inches by 10⅝ inches
E — 2¾ inches by 16¼ inches
F — 2¾ inches by 26½ inches
G — 2¾ inches by 32 inches
H— 8 inches by 32 inches
I — 8 inches by 48 inches

Assembly instructions:

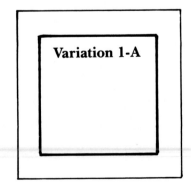

See Border Application Diagram, pg. 23.

How To Make an Amish Quilt

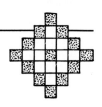

Variation 3

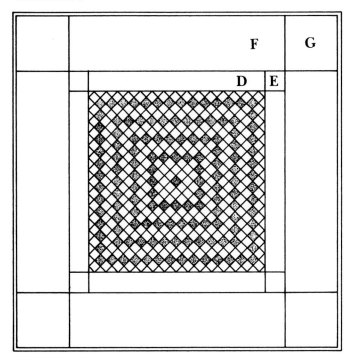

F G

D E

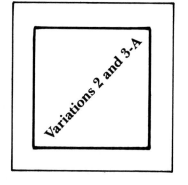

Variations 2 and 3-A

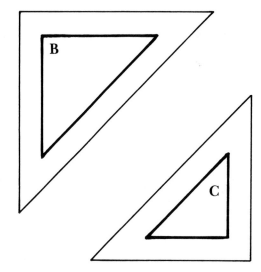

B

C

Measurements given <u>without</u> seam allowance

A — square template given
B — triangle template given
C — triangle template given
D — 3 inches x 26¼ inches
E — 3 inches square
F — 8 inches x 32¼
G — 8 inches square

Assembly instructions:

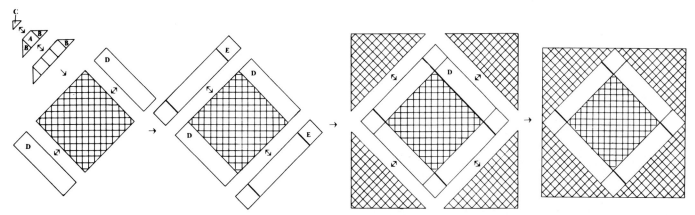

See Border Application Diagram, pg. 23.

Bars

Bars is a pattern of stark simplicity — straight vertical pieces surrounded by a border. There may be only two colors used alternately or an assortment of colors differing in each vertical bar.

Although it does appear among the midwestern Amish, the Bars pattern is a simple, plain one and was made largely among the Pennsylvania Amish. These quilts usually have wide borders covered with generous quilting, typical of Pennsylvania Amish quilts.

The most basic Bars quilt lacks any ornamentation other than the quilting designs, but variations of the Bars pattern exemplify the spirit of adventure and exploration found among this outwardly austere people.

The Split Bars variation adds interest by splitting the larger bands of color with additional narrow bands. Some quilters added a pieced inner border, while others created patterns within the bars themselves. The Wild Goose Chase pattern, for example, has a series of triangles ascending and descending the bars, giving the illusion of birds in flight. And a collection of Nine Patch blocks can be stacked inside the bars to give a more interesting design.

Bars, c. 1890-1900. Wool, 72 x 87. Lancaster Co., Pennsylvania. William B. Wigton.

The quilting designs on a Bars quilt more than adequately compensates for what may seem to be cold, stark piecing. The entire inner section of bars is sometimes treated as a whole and quilted in continuous lines of small even diamonds or some graceful, flowing design. Or each bar may be quilted in its own motif, giving a sampling of many different quilting designs. The open borders create a challenge for any avid quilter to use an abundance of feathers, cables, or other delicately stitched patterns.

It is not possible to make definitive statements about the inspiration for such a quilt design. However, it is likely that a people so close to the earth would be inclined to incorporate patterns of the field and the garden into other areas of life. One only needs observe a few of the meticulous gardens and fields of the Old Order Amish to see their pride in strong, straight lines. Plowed furrows in long even stretches, horizontal slats on wooden fences, or tobacco barns with opened vents could have provided the impetus for an Amish woman to create the Bars quilt.

Harvest is a time for thanksgiving. The Bars quilt pattern is reflected in this evening photo and the quilting motif is parallel to the rows of stubble.

How To Make an Amish Quilt

Bars, 1910-20. Cotton, 78 x 73. Lancaster Co., Pennsylvania. The People's Place, Intercourse, Pennsylvania.

How To Make an Amish Quilt

Bars
Approximate size 97 x 97

Variation 1

Measurements given <u>without</u> seam allowance
A — 8½ inches by 57¾ inches
B — 4¾ inches by 57¾ inches
C — 4¾ inches square
D — 15 inches by 67¼ inches
E — 15 inches square

Variation 2

Measurements given <u>without</u> seam allowance
A — 9½ inches by 66½ inches
B — 15 inches by 66½ inches
C — 15 inches square

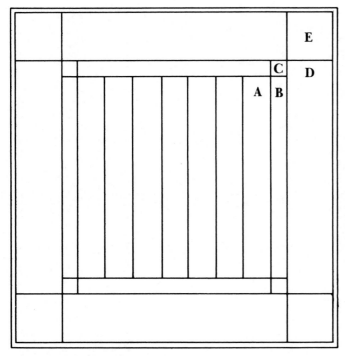
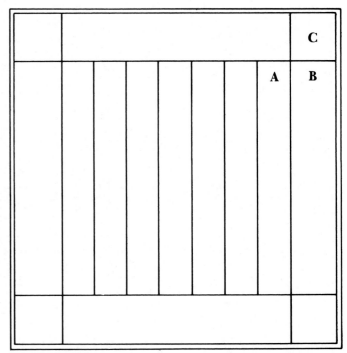

Assembly instructions:

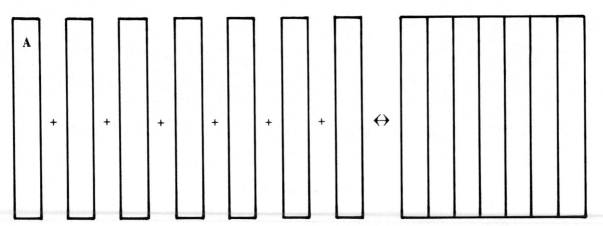

See Border Application Diagram, pg. 23.

How To Make an Amish Quilt

Wild Goose Chase Variation

Measurements given <u>without</u> seam allowance

A — triangle template given
B — triangle template given
C — 9 inches by 90 inches
D — 3 inches by 72 inches
E — 3 inches by 96 inches
F — 8 inches by 78 inches
G — 8 inches by 112 inches

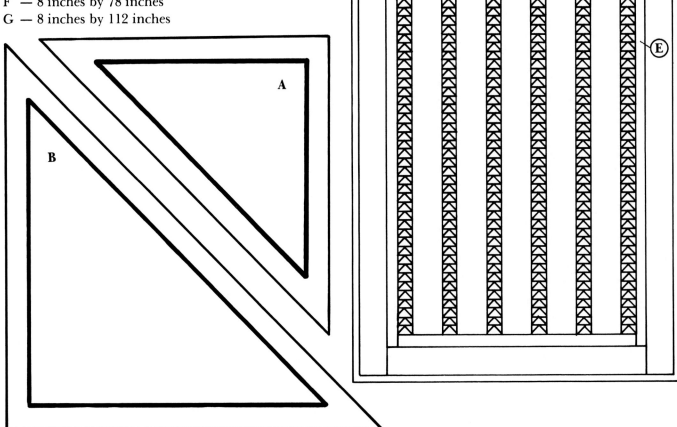

Assembly instructions:

See Border Application Diagram, **pg. 23.**

Bars
Approximate size 48 x 48

Variation 1

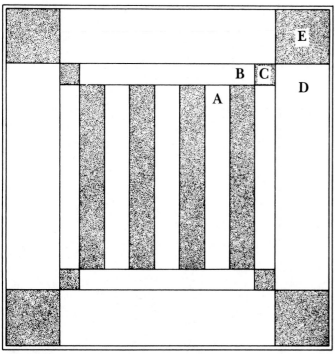

Variation 2

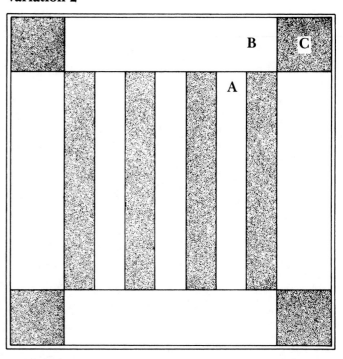

Measurements given <u>without</u> seam allowance
A — 3¾ inches by 26¼ inches
B — 3 inches by 26¼ inches
C — 3 inches square
D — 8 inches by 32½ inches
E — 8 inches square

Measurements given <u>without</u> seam allowance
A — 4½ inches by 31½ inches
B — 8 inches by 31½ inches
C — 8 inches square

Assembly instructions:

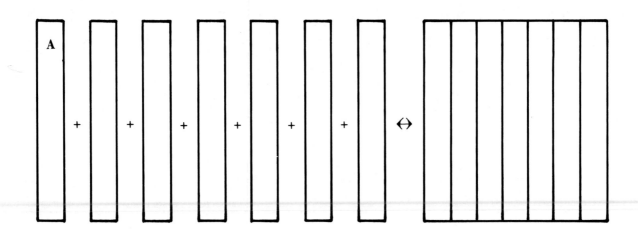

See Border Application Diagram, pg. 23.

How To Make an Amish Quilt

Wild Goose Chase Variation   Approximate size 43½ x 58

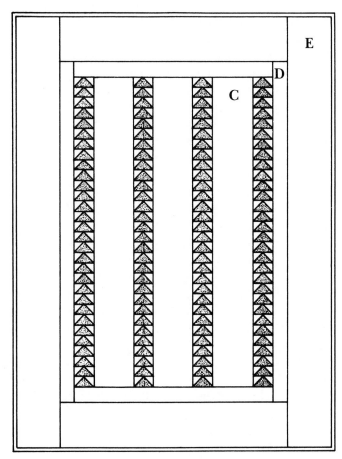

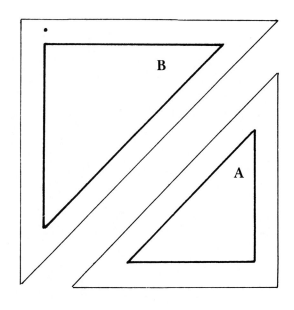

Assembly instructions:

Measurements given <u>without</u> seam allowance

A — triangle template given
B — triangle template given
C — 5½ inches by length of pieced strips
D — 2 inches by width of pieced interior
E — width of outer border 6 inches

See Border Application Diagram, pg. 23.

Multiple Patch Quilts

Blockwork, c. 1910. Glazed cotton, 67 x 73. Holmes Co., Ohio. Judi Boisson Antique American Quilts, New York. This pattern looks like a collection of miniature center diamond blocks collected and set together into one quilt.

This grouping covers a range of quilts from the simple One Patch pattern to the more complex Double Nine Patch, with variations on all these designs.

The One Patch is just what its name implies—a quilt made up of a series of single patches sewn together in a random or an organized fashion. The Four Patch is a series of blocks consisting of small patches in groups of four. The Double Four Patch uses a set of two four-patch blocks pieced with two solid patches the size of the quartet patch to form a square of four blocks. A series of these "double-four" blocks are sewn together, with sashing setting each square of four blocks apart.

The Nine Patch is the same idea worked in a series of threes. Nine small patches (three horizontal by three vertical patches) are sewn together to make a square. The Double Nine Patch uses five of these nine-square patches pieced together with four solid patches the size of the nine-patch to form a larger nine-patch combination. These large Double Nine Patches are sewn together, often separated by sashing to form the quilt top. Variations include the Four Patch in a Nine Patch, Nine Patch, or Four Patch in a Block Work.

The pattern is a simple one but the many possibilities allowed within the patches make it intriguing. Seldom are all the patches within a quilt done in the same color scheme. This multitude of color differences makes this a quilt with a sparkling potential.

Because of the small pieces and numerous color possibilities, it is an excellent pattern for a "scrap quilt." Any small snippet or scrap can be worked in at some spot.

This pattern was likely a first choice for many girls beginning their piecing skills. The simple straight lines make it easy to piece but the size and number of patches create enough challenge for a novice to tackle it with pride.

It is not only a beginner's quilt, however. The magnificent craftsmanship found in many of these quilts shows they are obviously the work of experienced and skilled hands.

The Amish are not opposed to education but they are cautious about too much formal training, especially in consolidated schools. The interplay of light and dark blocks in this Amish school is similar to the geometry in Multiple Patch quilts.

How To Make an Amish Quilt

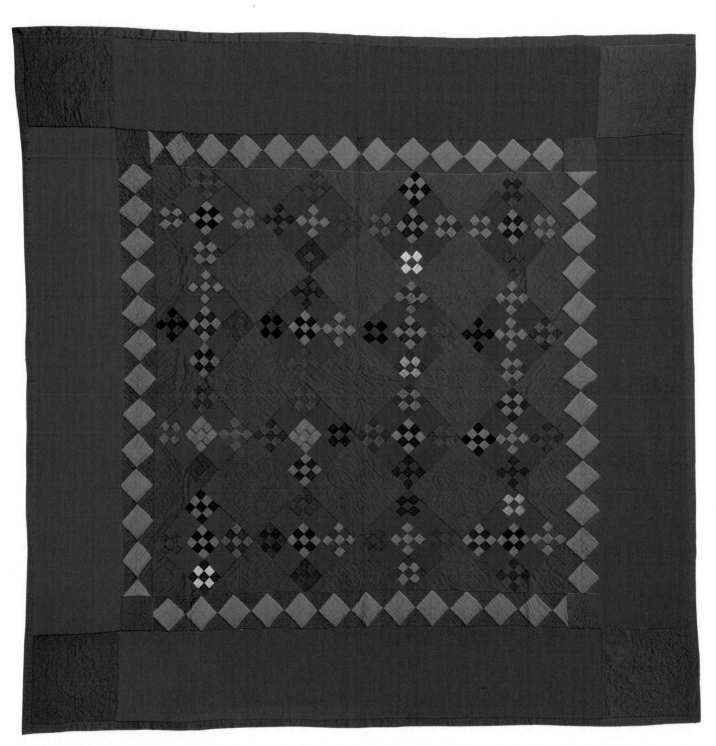

Double Nine Patch, c. 1930. Cotton, 83 x 82. Lancaster Co., Pennsylvania. Jay M. and Susen E. Leary. A pieced inner border of bright colors adds interest to this pattern.

Multiple Patch

Approximate size 96 x 118

Variation 1 — Double 9-Patch

Measurements given _without_ seam allowance

A — template given
B — template given
C — cut 6 squares 15¾ inches by 15¾
D — cut 10 triangles

15¾ inches
15¾ inches

E — cut 4 triangles

12½ inches
12½ inches

F — width of inner border 2⅝ inches
G — width of outer border 12 inches

Make 12 pieced blocks

Assembly instructions:

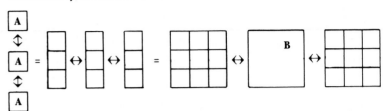

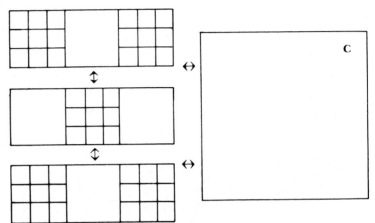

See Diagram 2, pg. 21 (Total Quilt Assembly).
See Border Application Diagram, pg. 23.

Double 4-Patch
Approximate size 96 x 104

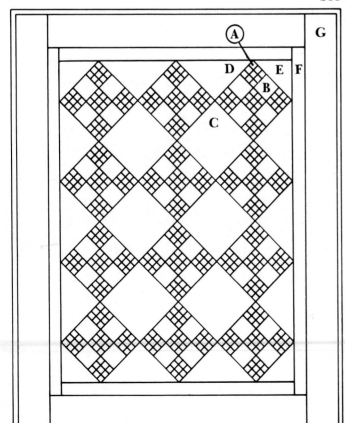

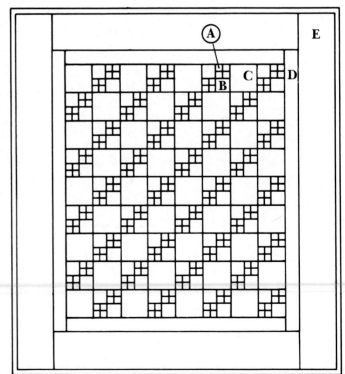

How To Make an Amish Quilt

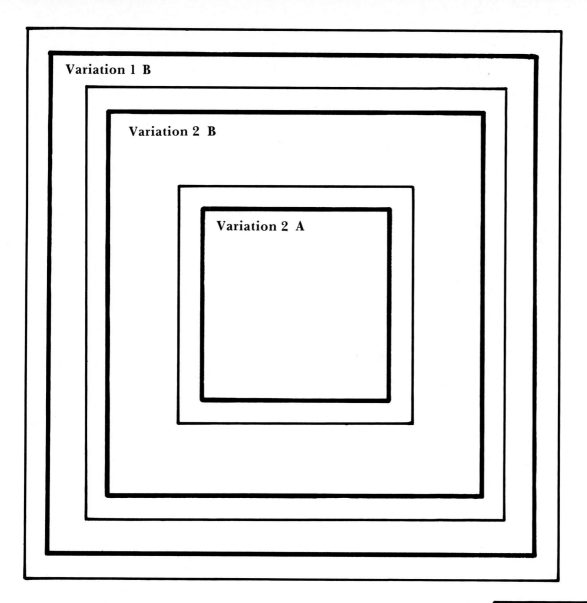

Variation 1 B

Variation 2 B

Variation 2 A

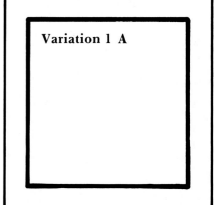

Variation 1 A

Variation 2 — Double 4-Patch

Measurements given <u>without</u> seam allowance

A — template given

B — template given

C — cut 36 squares 8 inches square

D — width of inner border — 3 inches

E — width of outer border — 13 inches

Make 20 pieced blocks

Assembly instructions:

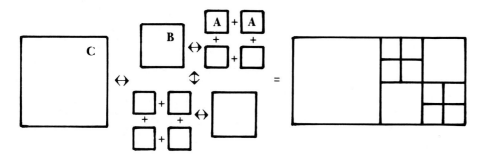

See Border Application Diagram, pg. 23.

How To Make an Amish Quilt

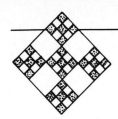

Multiple Patch
Approximate size 46 x 58

Variation 1—Double 9-Patch

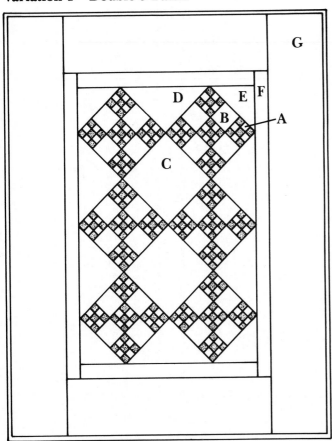

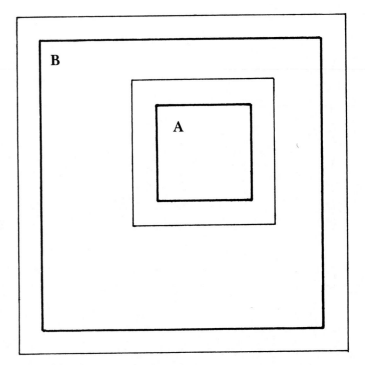

Measurements given <u>without</u> seam allowance

A— template given
B— template given
C— cut 2–9 inch squares
D— cut 6 triangles

9 inches
9 inches

E— cut 4 triangles

6⅜ inches
6⅜ inches

F— width of inner border 3 inches
G— width of outer border 8 inches

Make 6 pieced blocks

Assembly instructions:

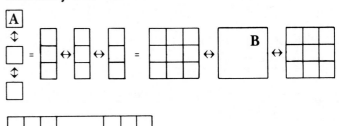

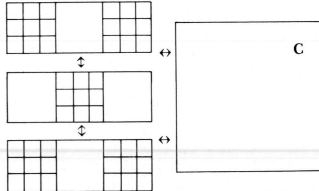

See Diagram 4, pg. 22 (Total Quilt Assembly).
See Border Application Diagram, pg. 23.

How To Make an Amish Quilt

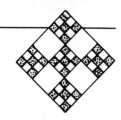

Variation 2—Double 4-Patch

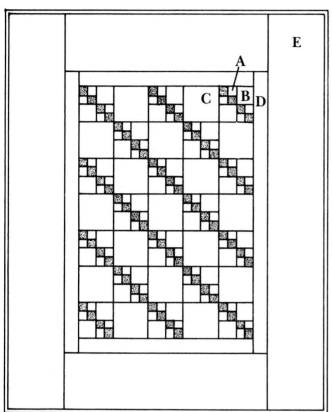

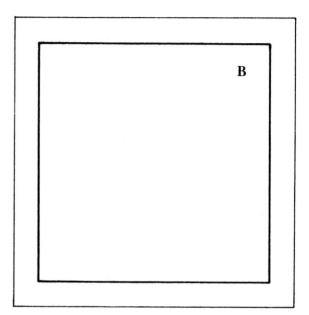

Measurements given <u>without</u> seam allowance

A— template given
B— template given
C— cut 17 squares 5 inches square
D— width of inner border—2 inches
E— width of outer border—8 inches

Make 18 pieced blocks

Assembly instructions:

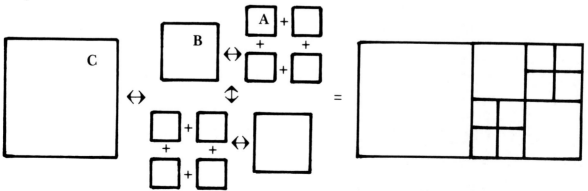

See Border Application Diagram, pg. 23.

How To Make an Amish Quilt

Irish Chain

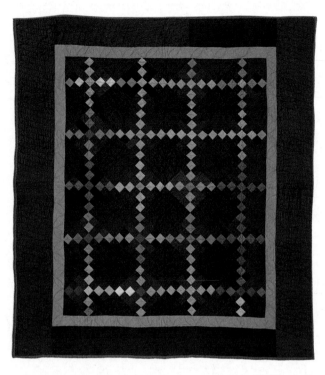

Single Irish Chain, c. 1920. Cotton, sateen, 64 x 70. Wayne Co., Ohio. William B. Wigton.

Here is a quilt with simple elegance — clear, sharp lines with ample space for generous quilting. The Irish Chain pattern can be pieced as a single row of blocks, a double row, or a triple row: the category is determined by the number of blocks creating the "chain" that runs diagonally or vertically through the quilt.

The single Irish Chain quilt can be constructed rather simply by making a series of simple Nine-Patch blocks in two colors. These are then tipped on their corners and sewn together alternately with solid squares of the same color to form the Single Irish Chain. Other variations of the pattern are much more complicated, requiring very careful placement of colors to create the chain effect.

The double and triple chain varieties often combine a bit of applique with the piecework. These patterns are sewn together so that a multiple patch is alternated with a solid patch of fabric the same size as the multiple patch. To achieve a consistent chain effect, small squares must be added to the corners of these solid patches. It is often easiest to applique those additional squares on top rather than trying to piece a right-angled corner.

The solid squares between the chain pattern as well as the typically wide borders on these quilts provide ample space for the outstanding quilting skills evident in Amish quilts. Curved, flowing quilting lines provide a contrast for the angles created by the pieced chain.

While the colors and fabrics used in Amish Irish Chain quilts make them distinctive, this is not a pattern unique to Amish quiltmakers. Irish Chain quilts were made by quilters in general. At some point, an Amish woman likely borrowed the pattern from a neighbor or friend and from there it probably circulated among Amish quilters.

These three girls are watching a game of baseball played on a Sunday afternoon in the neighbor's meadow. The fence pattern reminds one of an Irish Chain quilt.

How To Make an Amish Quilt

Triple Irish Chain, c. 1920. Cotton, 72 x 88. Mifflin Co., Pennsylvania. William B. Wigton.

Irish Chain
Approximate size 95 x 105

Measurements given <u>without</u> seam allowance

A — template given
B — cut 20 squares 8¾ x 8¾
C — cut 18 triangles

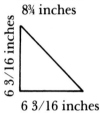

8¾ inches

8¾ inches

D — cut 4 triangles

6 3/16 inches

6 3/16 inches

E — width of inner border 3½ inches
F — width of outer border 12 inches

Make 30 pieced blocks
Plain blocks and triangles need template A and partial template A appliqued in the corners to complete the pattern.

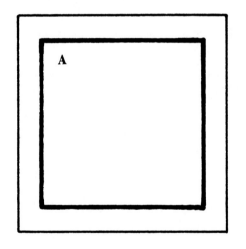

A

Variation 1 — Double Irish Chain

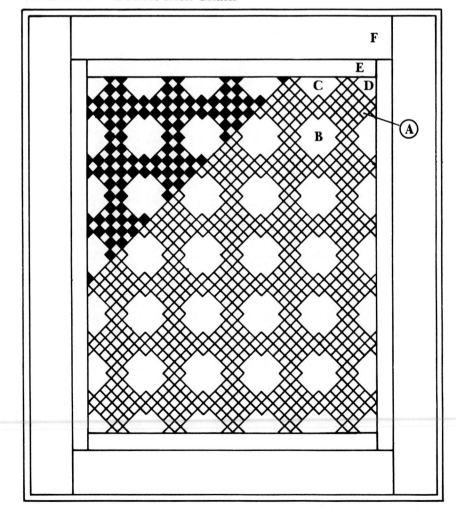

Assembly instructions:

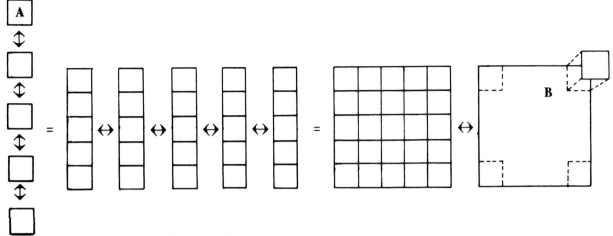

See Diagram 2, pg. 21 (Total Quilt Assembly).
See Border Application Diagram, pg. 23.

Variation 2 — Single Irish Chain
Proceed as in Variation 1 but eliminate appliqued
squares on plain alternate blocks.

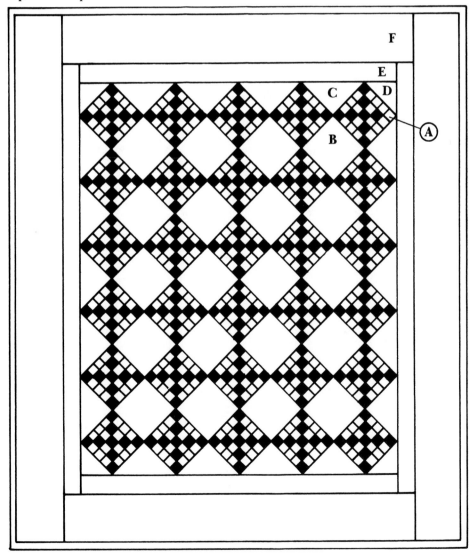

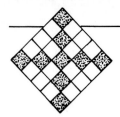

Irish Chain
Approximate size 47 x 55

Variation 1—Double Irish Chain

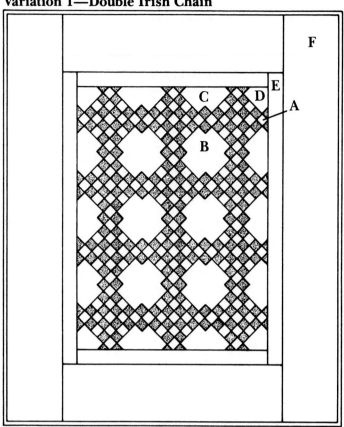

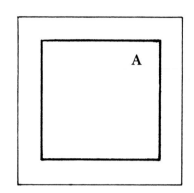

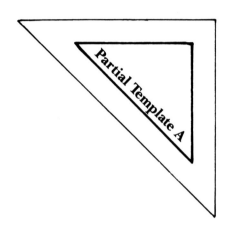

Measurements given <u>without</u> seam allowance

A — template given
B — cut 6-6¼ inch squares
C — cut 10 triangle

6¼ inches
6¼ inches

D — cut 4 triangles

4⅜ inches
4⅜ inches

E — width of inner border 2 inches
F — width of outer border 8 inches

Make 12 pieced blocks
Plain blocks and triangles need template A and
partial template A appliqued in the corners to
complete the pattern.

Assembly instructions:

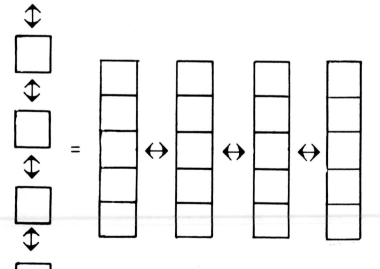

How To Make an Amish Quilt

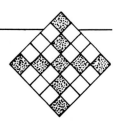

Variation 2—Single Irish Chain

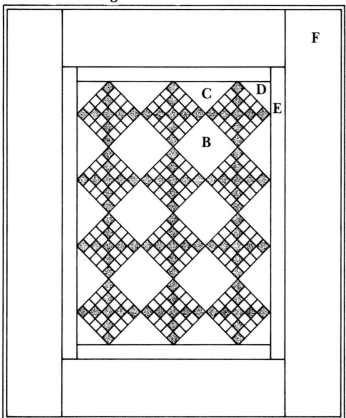

Proceed as in Variation 1 but eliminate appliqued squares on plain alternate blocks.

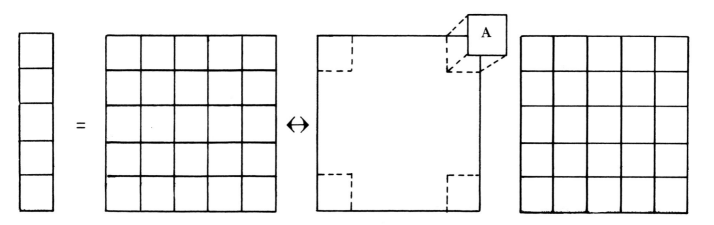

See Diagram 4, pg. 22 (Total Quilt Assembly).
See Border Application Diagram, pg. 23.

Though simple, Amish houses are warm and friendly. Attention is given to cleanliness and order.

Color Among the Amish

Probably the most distinctive quality about Amish quilts is their color. Other quilters from the past would on occasion use exclusively solid fabrics. But Amish women consistently used only solid colors for their quilts. Most antique quilts are made from fabric scraps, usually left over from other sewing projects. Since much Amish clothing, especially women's dresses, men's shirts, and children's clothing, has traditionally been made at home, it is the fabric left from these handmade dresses and shirts that create the vivid, deep colors found in Amish quilts.

Amish clothing at a quick glance seems dark and somber because of its heavy use of black. But children's clothing and young women's dresses are gaily colored blues, greens, purples, pinks and dark reds. Although the styles are conservative (children wear miniature models of adult clothing), the colors are bold and bright. The colors, it seems, match the children's energies.

"Naive" Color Combinations

Amish quilts are also generally spoken of as "dark." However, there are few quilts as daring and bold in color as those made by the Amish. How can this seeming paradox

be explained? Amish quiltmakers, because of their limited access to color and fashion trends, work in a nearly uninhibited color world. Most children in the larger society begin early in their lives to subconsciously develop a color sense. Their socks match their pants; their pants match their shirt; their sweaters are coordinated. All this takes place in homes where carpets, draperies, and walls are synchronized with accessories and furnishings.

In an Amish setting, one style of clothing is worn and only part of its color changes from day to day. One never need worry about whether one's pink dress matches one's black stockings and black shoes. Most Amish homes do not contain upholstered furniture, their walls are generally painted a solid blue or green, and carpets, where found, are often hand-woven rag rugs. This lack of color consciousness among the Amish leaves them completely open to the possible use of fabrics from their scrap bag.

Amish women were not told that color hues vary depending on their reference point. But they could see—and feel—it happening. Numerous quilts were pieced without the maker's knowledge of the science of what she was doing. She saw it and knew inherently that the two colors brought out the best in each other. For example, many

How To Make an Amish Quilt

antique Amish quilts have touches of black and red, two choices which add spark to nearly any color scheme. Amish women simply recognized it as a pleasing combination. Their approach to color was new, fresh, and followed gut-level instincts. Perhaps that is why these quilts have such wide appeal. Everyone's creative sense knows when something is correct, but too often the "modern" person knows too much to make these free decisions.

Clothing Colors Used Primarily

Among the Old Order Amish there were and are stipulations about clothing colors. The more conservative groups of Eastern Pennsylvania avoid red, red-orange, orange, and yellow. But burgundy hues are permitted. Amish groups in Mifflin County, Pennsylvania, use many bright, gaudy colors including yellows. Midwestern Amish also tend to allow bright and varied clothing colors.

Occasionally a "stray" color appears in an antique Amish quilt. One Amish woman explained how these color exceptions may have happened: midwestern Amish women often bought fabrics from peddlers who went from home to home with their wares. A good peddler learned to know his territory and how to market his merchandise. He knew what kinds of fabrics appealed to his Amish clients and made bundles of those fabrics offering them at a bargain rate. But among the desirables he might place some pieces that were slow movers. One Amish woman wanted a bundle of fabrics that contained a piece of bright red cloth. Knowing that this particular color was out of her domain, she explained to the peddler that she would like the bundle but with an exchange for the red. Apparently having had trouble moving the red elsewhere, he refused to swap. So she purchased, along with her needs, a piece that she could use only in a secondary function. This bright red cloth became quilt fabric.

Some Quilt Fabrics Purchased

Not all old quilts are made from scraps. Large sections of fabrics used for backings and borders needed to be purchased. But the principle of frugality is strong among these people. So remnant shopping and bargain hunting for fabrics was likely common and would account for some of the exceptional colors used. Backings were sometimes printed fabrics even though prints are seldom permitted for clothing.

These old quilts delight and surprise the viewer with their vibrance and lasting beauty. They bridge the gap from a separate people to the modern world. Their beauty, though perhaps understood in different ways by each group, is loved and appreciated by both.

Vivid juxtaposition of color in the Amish world is common. Somber dress intensifies the spritely colors for which Amish quilts are well known.

Many Amish are employed at home on the farm. As a result, parents and children spend more time together than in families where one or both parents drive to work.

How To Make an Amish Quilt

Log Cabin

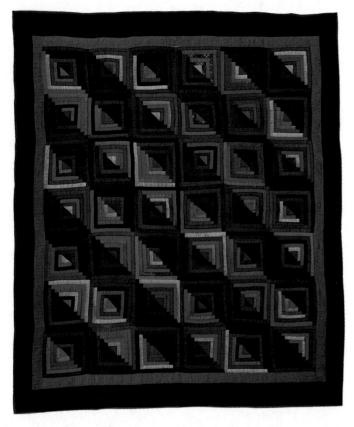

Log Cabin — Diagonal Furrows Variation, c. 1900-10. Wool, 66 x 78. Mifflin Co. Pennsylvania. William and Connie Hayes.

Mutual aid is a way of life for the Amish. Barn raisings are common in Amish settlements, both in the actual construction of barns and in the Log Cabin quilt pattern.

A favorite with quiltmakers in general, the Log Cabin also thrived among Amish quilters. Its possibilities are almost infinite. There are Barn Raising, Courthouse Steps, Straight Furrows, and Pineapple or Windmill Blades variations. And each of those can be made with solid borders, pieced borders, or no border at all.

The Log Cabin quilt is often a scrap quilt. Its narrow "log"-shaped pieces in varying lengths could accommodate many scraps that were not large enough for other patterns. Perhaps this is why so many Log Cabin quilts flourish in so many diverse constructions.

Assembly of this quilt is straightforward. It begins with a center square upon which the "logs" are stacked. The first is the length of the square. The block is then rotated one-quarter turn and the next log (the length of the square plus the previous log) is added. This continues with varying numbers of logs to form the basic log cabin patch.

Patches are often arranged with light fabrics on one half of the block and dark fabrics on the other half, which when sewn together, produce a larger pattern on the quilt top.

The visual images are apparent. One can see the sun streaming through the rafters of a barn under construction. Straight furrows are sharp and clear and the dark patches conjure up images of rich, dark soil waiting to burst forth with harvest. The tiny steps of the logs create the Courthouse Steps, and the Windmill Blades variation seems to spin as easily as the windmill pumping water on an Amish farm.

Log Cabin quilts are one of the exceptions to the general rule of elaborate quilting on Amish quilts. These quilts are sometimes quilted only on the borders, sometimes not at all. In some cases the quilt top, lining, and backing are connected in the piecing process. The blocks are then sewn together, eliminating the functional need for quilting. In other cases, quilts are "tied" or "knotted" (tacked with heavy string at regular intervals) rather than quilted. That may have been done because the narrow width of the logs creates the problem of having to quilt through a seam allowance, thus making quilting less pleasurable and less fine. When Log Cabin patterns are quilted, the stitching is usually minimal in the pieced part of the quilt and more abundant on the borders.

How To Make an Amish Quilt

Log Cabin, c. 1890-1900. Wool, 82 x 84. Mifflin Co., Pennsylvania. William B. Wigton. A strong contrast in colors makes the barn raising design in this quilt very obvious. The pieced borders continue the theme of narrow strips.

How To Make an Amish Quilt

Log Cabin
Approximate size 96 x 108

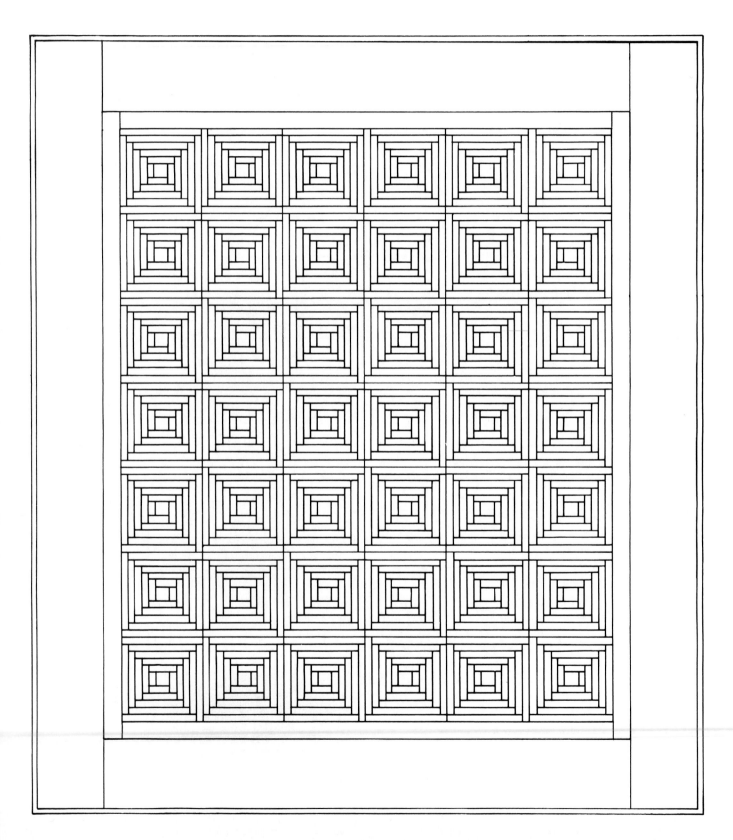

How To Make an Amish Quilt

Assembly instructions:

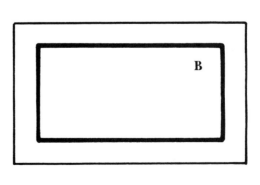

$$A \leftrightarrow B = \boxed{} \rightarrow C \leftrightarrow \boxed{} = \boxed{} = \boxed{} \leftrightarrow D \quad \text{etc.}$$

See Border Application Diagram, pg. 23.

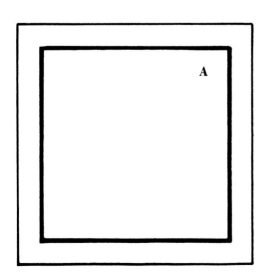

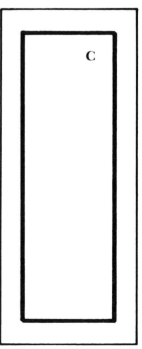

D

E

F

G

H

How To Make an Amish Quilt

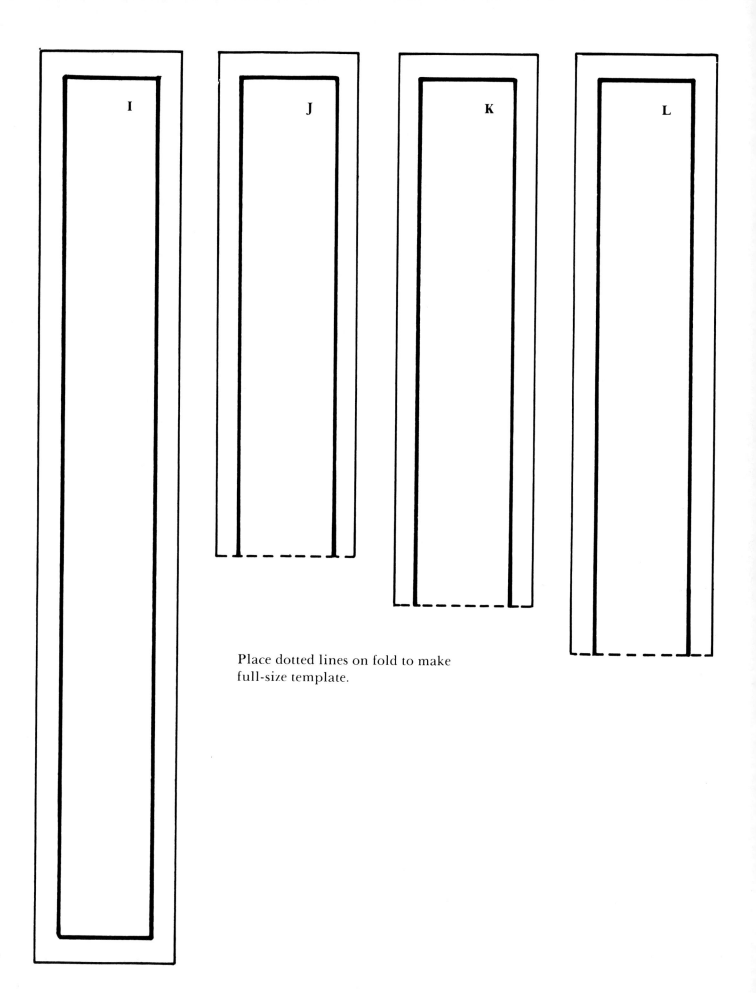

I

J

K

L

Place dotted lines on fold to make
full-size template.

Log Cabin
Approximate size 45 x 53

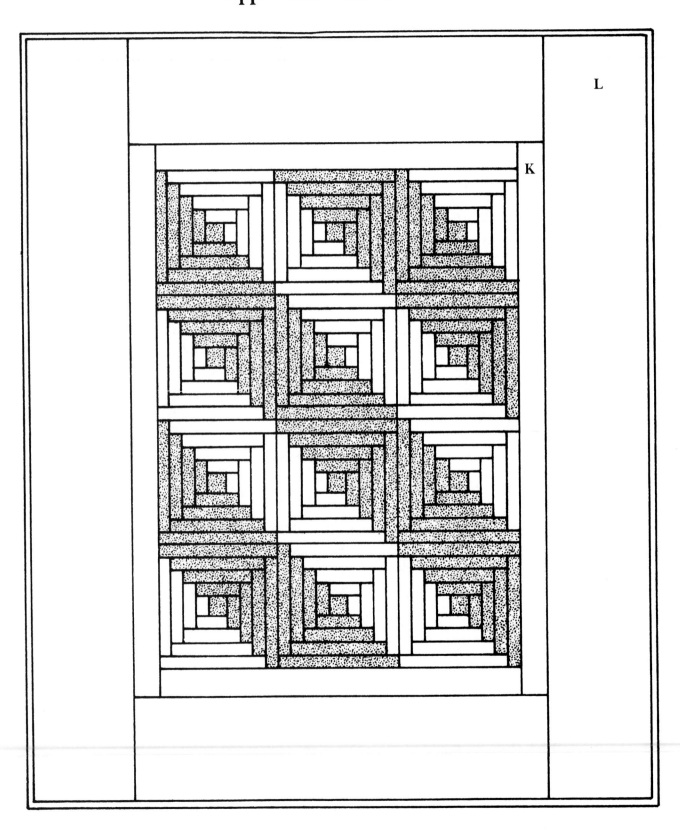

Assembly instructions:

K—width of inner border 2 inches
L—width of outer border 8 inches

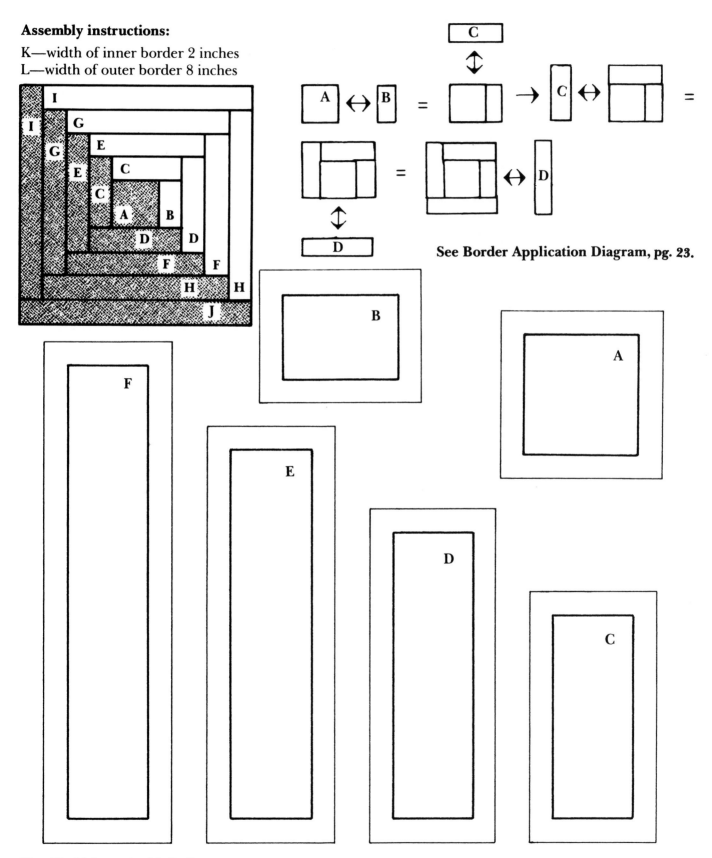

See Border Application Diagram, pg. 23.

G

H

I

J

How To Make an Amish Quilt

Double T

It is often difficult to document how patterns were developed or named. The Double T, however, looks like what it is called — a T that mirrors itself in two directions. Perhaps this particular pattern began as a Nine Patch (see the center of the Double T patch).

This pattern is seldom found among Amish quilts of Pennsylvania. It is a Midwestern quilt pattern, perhaps learned by an Amish woman from a neighbor. There seems to have been much more borrowing by the Midwestern Amish of patterns from outside their community; at least, these Amish used many more patterns than did the Pennsylvania Amish. Perhaps the same spirit of adventure and necessity that allowed Amish families to move West is reflected in their more experimental attitudes in quiltmaking.

Quilting is an integral part of most Amish quilts. This pattern is no exception. Borders and open blocks between piecework encourage the abundance of stitching that helps make these quilts the masterpieces they are.

Double T, c. 1920. Cotton, 80 x 70. Northern Indiana. Nancy Meng.
A triple inside border and generous quilting add to the beauty of the quilt.

Detail of above quilt.
Note the subtle color variations in this dichromatic quilt.

Double T
Approximate size 96 x 111

Measurements given <u>without</u> seam allowance

A — template given
B — template given
C — template given
D — cut 20 squares 10½ x 10½ inches
E — cut 18 triangles

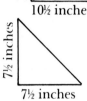

10½ inches / 10½ inches

F — cut 4 triangles

7½ inches / 7½ inches

G — width of inner border 2 inches
H — width of outer border 9 inches
Make 30 pieced blocks

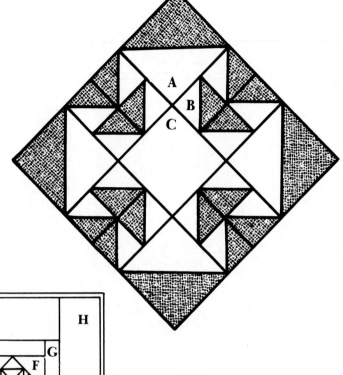

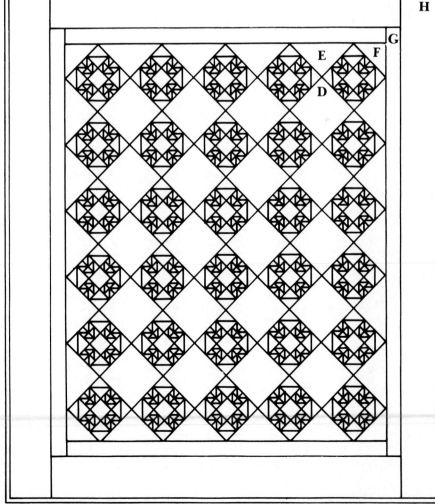

Assembly instructions:

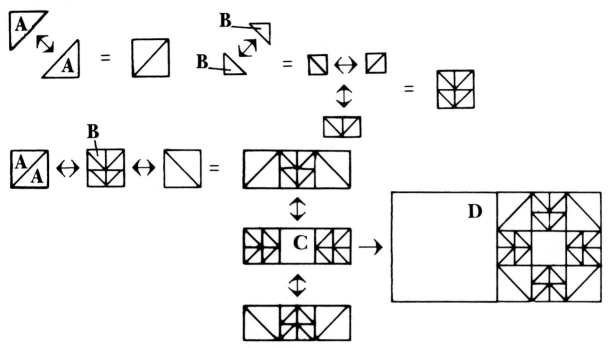

See Diagram 2, pg. 21 (Total Quilt Assembly).
See Border Application Diagram, pg. 23.

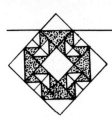

Double T
Approximate size 46 x 58

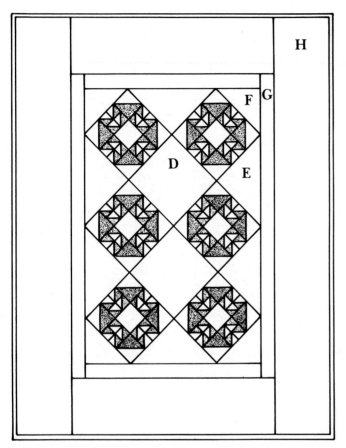

Measurements given <u>without</u> seam allowance

A — template given
B — template given
C — template given
D — cut 2–9 inch squares
E — cut 6 triangles

9 inches
9 inches

F — cut 4 triangles

6⅜ inches
6⅜ inches

G — width of inner border 2 inches
H — width of outer border 8 inches
Make 6 pieced blocks

How To Make an Amish Quilt

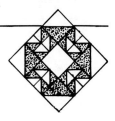

Assembly instructions:

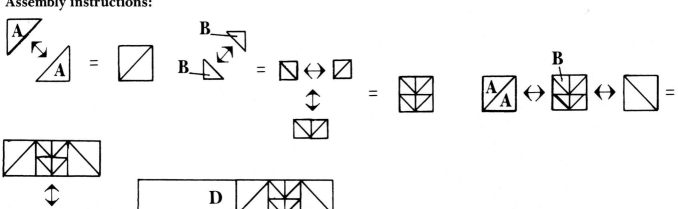

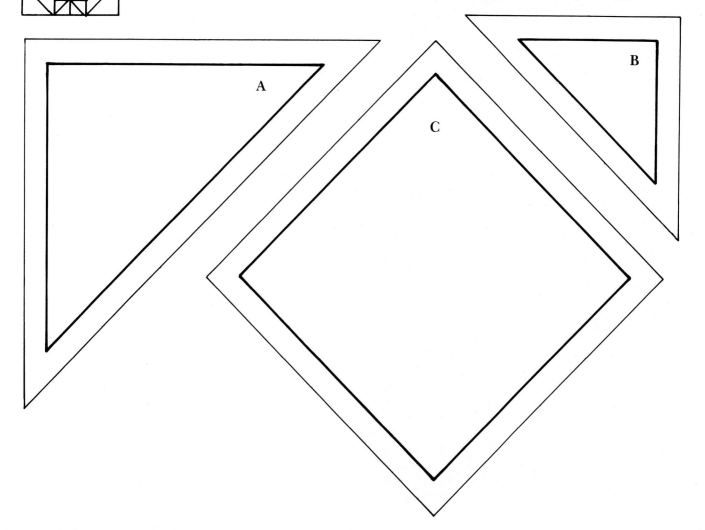

See Diagram 4, pg. 22 (Total Quilt Assembly).
See Border Application Diagram, pg. 23.

Stars

Broken Star, c. 1920-30. Cotton, 85 x 85. Ohio. Judi Boisson Antique American Quilts, New York. The use of the tiny nine patch blocks bring together the corners of the triple inside border. Fiddlehead ferns are quilted throughout the border.

Star motifs are common in Amish quilts and handcrafts. Perhaps this intrigue with heavenly bodies stems from their day's work, beginning and ending at the bidding of the sun.

Numerous quilt patterns deal with the heavenly bodies. Perhaps this fascination with the sky stems from the fact that so much of rural life begins and ends at the bidding of the sun.

The rising and setting sun are particularly important in an Amish home. Without electric lights, sewing is frequently done inside a window where one can reap the full benefit of the sun's light. While gas lamps provide ample light for reading or a game of checkers, the coming of darkness brings rest and the time for work to cease.

Probably the most dramatic of the star quilt patterns are the Lone Star and the Broken Star. In these, a large star seems to burst from the center of the quilt, sending light to the ends of its eight points. In the Broken Star, the additional energy of a pieced border surrounding the central star causes the pattern to appear to pulsate.

Successful construction of these quilts requires meticulous accuracy in cutting and piecing the small diamonds. A minute error will be numerously multiplied when trying to match the diamonds' corners in this magnificent quilt.

Quilting adds another striking feature to these already dramatic bedcovers. Open corners surrounding the stars and wide outer borders seem always to inspire fresh energy and imagination in quilters. This ornamental stitching adds depth and grace to the quilt.

Star quilts come in an abundance of shapes and sizes. In addition to the large star patterns there are many smaller star designs worked in a series of blocks.

One of the features that make the Amish star quilts so outstanding is their fabrics. Many of these star quilts have backgrounds of a very dark color, making the star itself seem to sparkle like the stars in a clear night sky.

Star patterns, although popular with quilters in general, seem to have been accepted and widely used by the Amish. It suggests a wonderful blending of their respect for God's creation and their love of beauty.

Broken Star, c. 1925-30. Cotton, 72 x 72. Ohio. William and Connie Hayes.

Stars
Approximate size 94 x 105

Variation 1 — Lone Star

Measurements given <u>without</u> seam allowance

A — template given

B — cut 4 squares 18 inches by 18 inches

C — cut 4 triangles

18 inches / 18 inches

D — cut 9 triangles

9 inches / 9 inches

E — cut 2 triangles

6 5/16 / 6 5/16 inches

F — width of border 16 inches

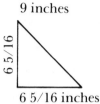

Assembly instructions:

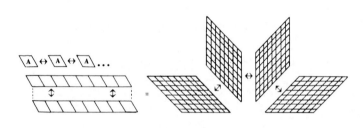

A ↔ A ↔ A ...

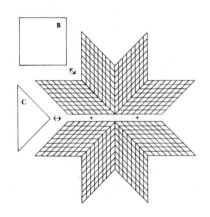

See Border Application Diagram, pg. 23.

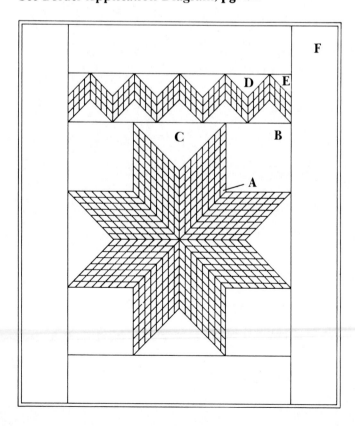

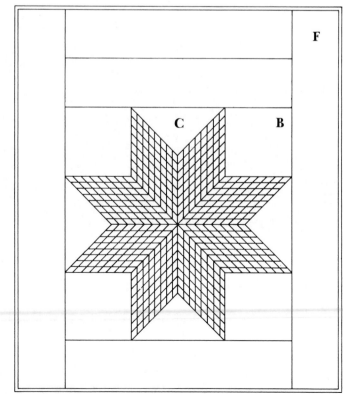

Variation 2 — Broken Star

Measurements given <u>without</u> seam allowance

A — template given (smaller than Variation 1)
B — cut 20 squares 9 inches by 9 inches
C — cut 8 triangles

D — cut 1 rectangle 12 inches by 61½ inches
E — width of border 16 inches

Assembly instructions:

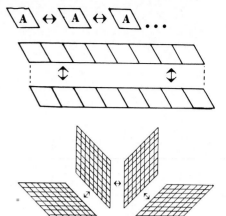

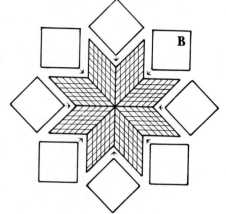

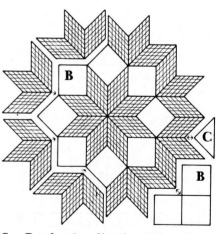

See Border Application Diagram, pg. 23.

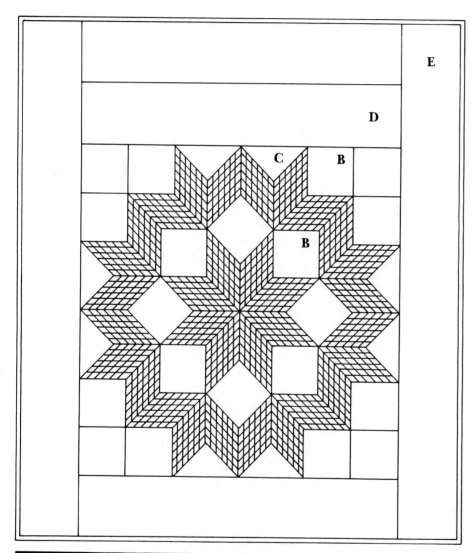

Stars
Approximate size 48 x 57

Variation 1—Lone Star

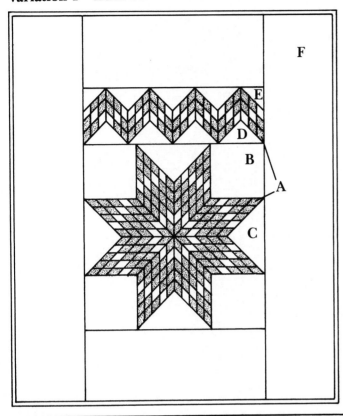

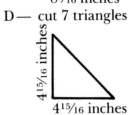

Measurements given <u>without</u> seam allowance

A — template given
B — cut 4 squares 8³⁄₁₆ inches by 8³⁄₁₆ inches
C — cut 4 triangles

8³⁄₁₆ inches / 8³⁄₁₆ inches

D — cut 7 triangles

4¹⁵⁄₁₆ inches / 4¹⁵⁄₁₆ inches

E — cut 2 triangles

3½ inches / 3½ inches

F — width of border 10 inches

Assembly instructions:

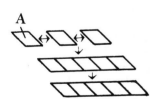

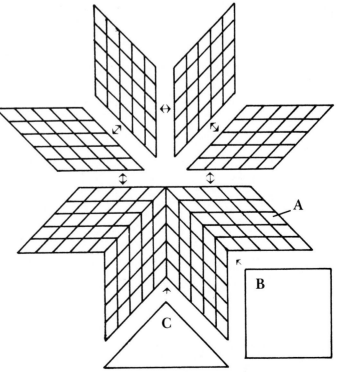

See Border Application Diagram, pg. 23.

How To Make an Amish Quilt

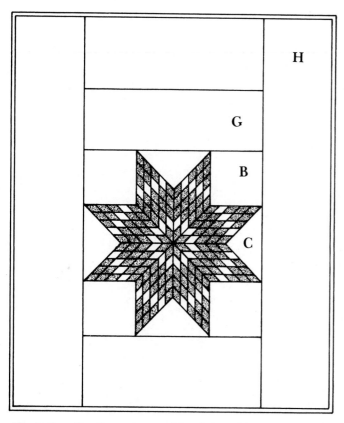

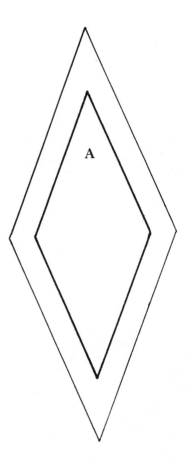

Variation 2—Lone star with plain pillow throw same as Variation 1 except eliminate D and E and replace with G-8½ x width of pieced star

Jacob's Ladder

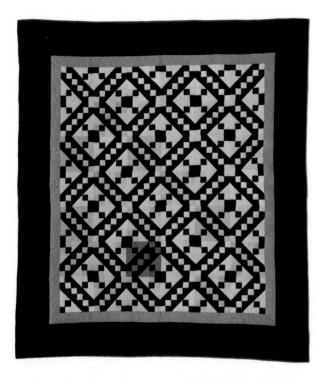

The Jacob's Ladder pattern was brought into the Amish community from outside. Its religious roots perhaps made it desirable to Amish women.

Jacob's Ladder depicts the ladder from the Old Testament story of Jacob's vision of angels ascending and descending from heaven to minister to him on earth.

Colors must be carefully arranged to execute this pattern correctly. The pattern is a series of four patch blocks and triangles arranged with light and dark fabrics to form continuous diagonals across the quilt surface.

Quilting on the pieced portion of this quilt is generally done in straight lines with more elaborate quilting on the borders.

Jacob's Ladder, c. 1920. Cotton, 68 x 80. Probably LaGrange Co., Indiana. Rebecca Haarer. One isolated blue patch wandered into the making of an otherwise subdued color scheme.

Detail of above quilt. A single patch in a quilt that stands alone in its color selection and combination is common in old Amish quilts.

How To Make an Amish Quilt

Jacob's Ladder
Approximate size 93 x 104

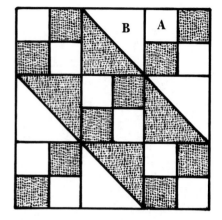

Measurements given <u>without</u> seam allowance

A — template given

B — template given

C — width of inner border 4 inches

D — width of outer border 11 inches

Make 42 pieced blocks

Assembly instructions:

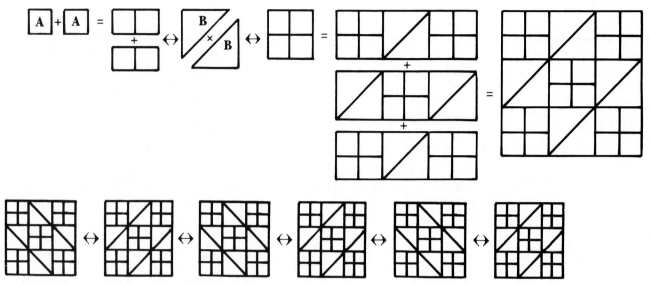

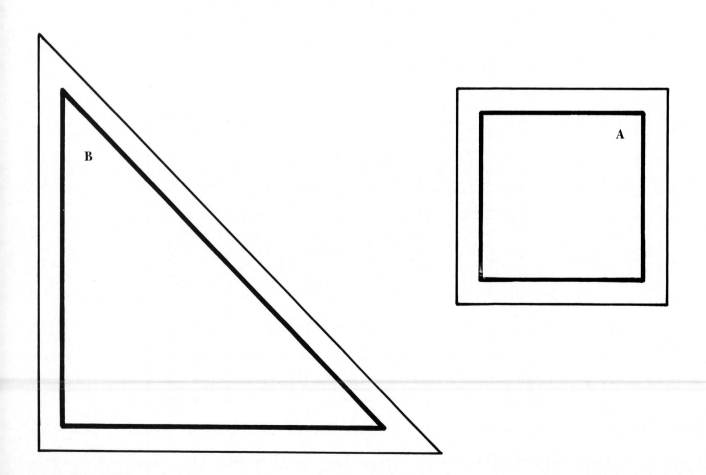

See Diagram 1, pg. 21 (Total Quilt Assembly).
See Border Application Diagram, pg. 23.

How To Make an Amish Quilt

Jacob's Ladder
Approximate size 44 x 58

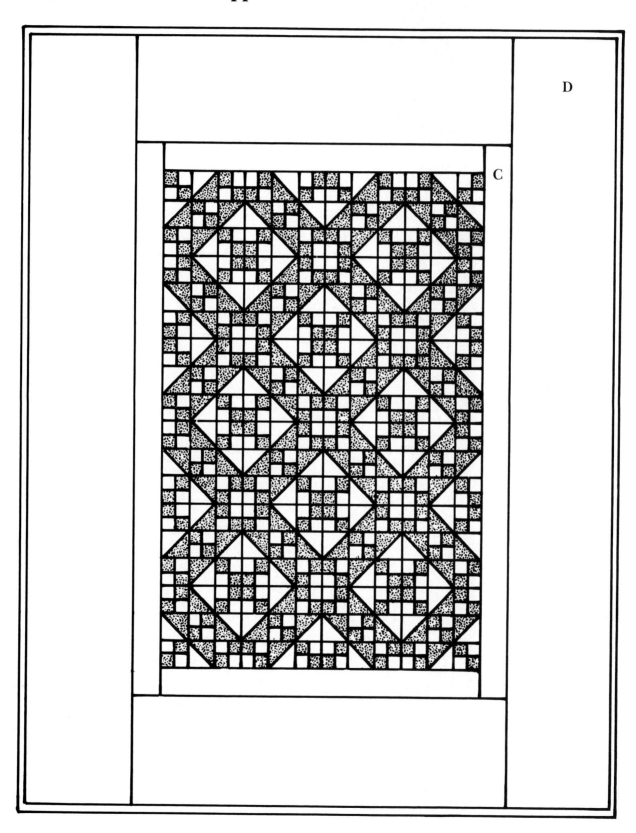

Measurements given <u>without</u> seam allowance

A — template given
B — template given
C — width of inner border 2 inches
D — width of outer border 8 inches

Make 24 pieced blocks

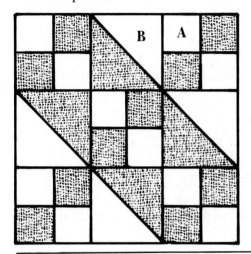

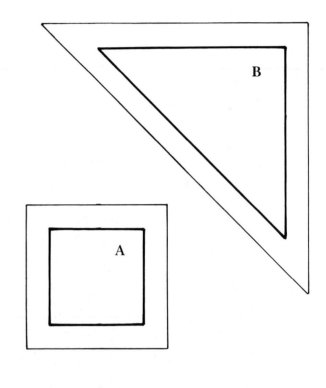

Assembly instructions:

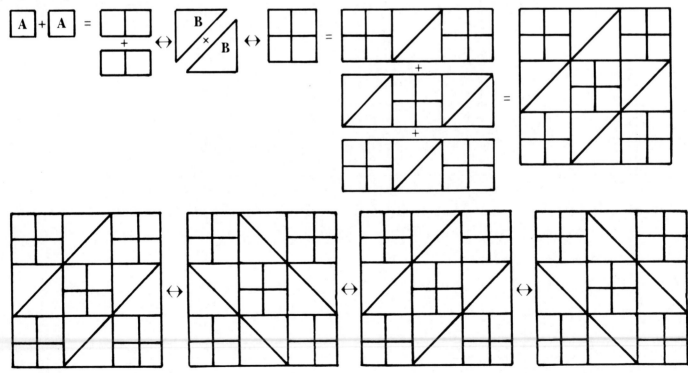

See Diagram 3, pg. 22 (Total Quilt Assembly).
See Border Application Diagram, pg. 23.

How To Make an Amish Quilt

Baskets

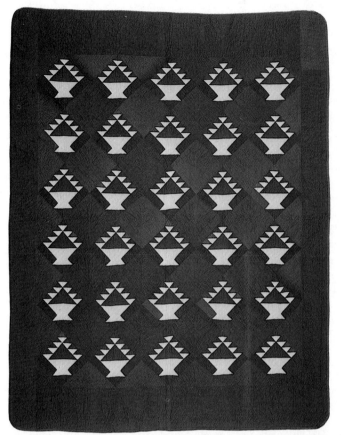

Amish Basket quilts come mainly from the Midwest where there was a comparatively more open approach to quiltmaking than among the Pennsylvania Amish. Baskets were popular in general society and the adoption of this pattern by Amish women is somewhat unusual, as Amish quilts tend to avoid the realistic reproduction of an object. There are, however, lovely examples of this design worked by Amish quilters.

Basket patterns use a variety of geometric shapes to create the finished image. Adequate and proper contrasting of fabrics is necessary to enhance the basket design. Where curved handles are a part of the basket, they are appliqued after the Basket block is completed.

The basket, as a design motif, is sometimes quilted on the borders of other quilt patterns. But it is seldom used as the quilting design on a pieced Basket quilt.

On a quilt top the basket blocks are usually alternated with solid blocks of the same size which are quilted with full, flowing lines. Borders provide additional space to display quilting expertise.

Baskets, c. 1910. Cotton, 86 x 66. Ohio. Judi Boisson Antique American Quilts, New York. Several shades of blue are contrasted with the hollow baskets. Tulips are quilted in the alternate plain blocks.

Baskets are common containers around Amish farms. Carrying produce from garden to house or from garden to market is often done in baskets.

Cactus Basket or Star Basket, 1940. Cotton, 75 x 92. Amherst, Wisconsin. Collection of Catherine H. Anthony. Perky baskets appear the same at first glance but study shows subtle differences in the fabrics of the inside petals.

Baskets, c. 1925. Glazed cotton, 92 x 67. Holmes Co., Ohio. Judi Boisson Antique American Quilts, New York. Baskets are pieced and handles appliqued for this pattern. Note the name embroidered on the inside border.

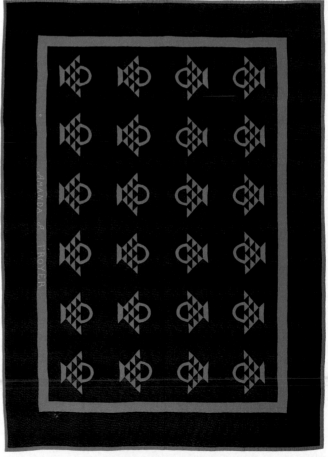

How To Make an Amish Quilt

Baskets, dated March 21, 1915 and 1945. Cotton, 84 x 61. LaGrange Co., Indiana. Rebecca Haarer. Baskets stand out sharply against a black background.

How To Make an Amish Quilt

Baskets
Approximate size 90 x 105

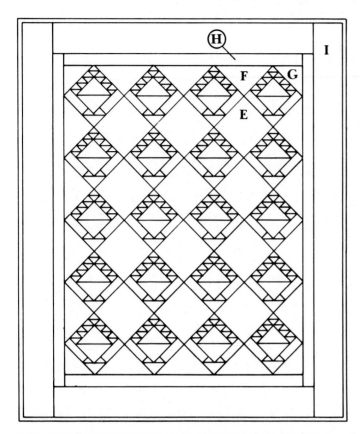

Measurements given <u>without</u> seam allowance
A — template given
B — template given
C — template given
D — template given
E — cut 12 squares 10½ by 10½ inches
F — cut 14 triangles

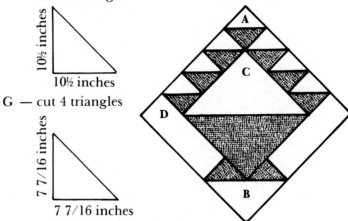

10½ inches / 10½ inches

G — cut 4 triangles

7 7/16 inches / 7 7/16 inches

H — width of inner border 3 inches
I — width of outer border 15 inches

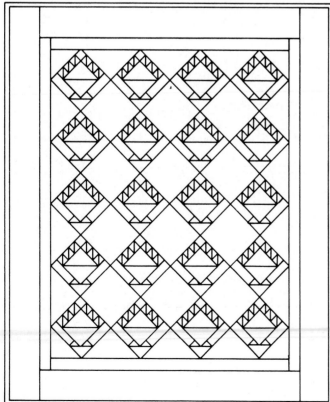

Assembly instructions:

See Diagram 2, pg. 21 (Total Quilt Assembly).
See Border Application Diagram, pg. 23.

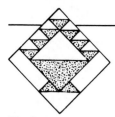

Baskets
Approximate size 46 x 58

Variation 1

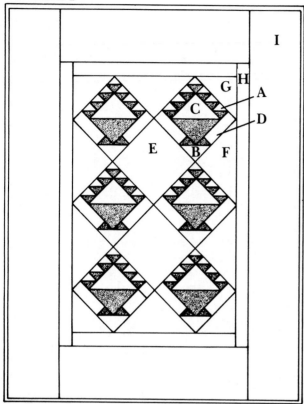

Variation 2

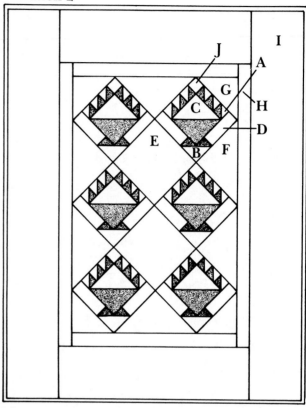

Variation 3

Measurements given <u>without</u> seam allowance

A — template given
B — template given
C — template given
D — template given
E — cut 2–9 inch squares
F — cut 6 triangles

9 inches / 9 inches

G — cut 4 triangles

$6\frac{3}{8}$ inches / $6\frac{3}{8}$ inches

H — width of inner border 2 inches
I — width of outer border 8 inches
J — template given (used in variations 2 and 3)

How To Make an Amish Quilt

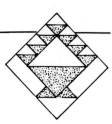

Assembly instructions:

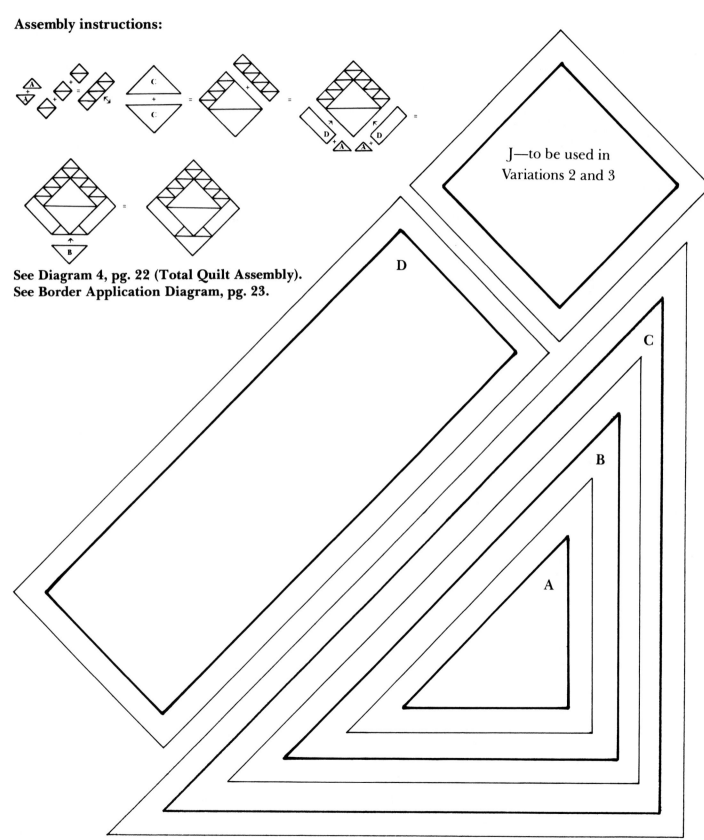

See Diagram 4, pg. 22 (Total Quilt Assembly).
See Border Application Diagram, pg. 23.

J—to be used in Variations 2 and 3

D

C

B

A

Children are loved and enjoyed in the Amish community. They grow up eating, drinking, playing and working "Amishness" and usually join the church as young adults.

Quilts in the Life Cycle

A people who live from the land know well its seasons and changes. And their own day-to-day lives flow in rhythm with the earth's movement.

The Earth Gives

Spring is the time for planting fields, gardens, and flower beds. Housecleaning gets underway with the women scrubbing the house from top to bottom, airing the mattresses, beating the rugs, wiping walls and ceilings, washing windows to a sparkle, and emptying and cleaning cupboards and drawers. With warmer weather comes vigor for these projects. There is a freshness in the air indoors and out. Lawns are raked free of debris and primped and prepared for the burst of color promised by newly planted flower beds.

Field work begins and ends with the sun. Men and those children no longer in school spend long days standing on the plow behind a team of horses. Their reward? The smell and texture of newly turned earth!

Summer and the closing of school bring extra hands to help hoe the corn, top tobacco, and cut and bale hay before the rain comes. It is a rushed time, but rich in the earth's plenty. There are strawberries to pick, peas to pod, beans to

shell and corn to be husked. There are new potatoes and tender asparagus to be collected. Cantaloupes, watermelons and fresh fruits offer themselves for snacks and desserts. Not only is there enough to fill summertime tables, but all the fruits have been planted in excess so as to be preserved for the winter months.

Fall comes and with it the children's return to school, the last of the harvest and quieter days on the farm. Fall housecleaning sweeps away the summer's clutter. Window screens are replaced with storm windows; hay mows and corn cribs are stacked full; silos burst with food for cattle during cold months. And when the days become shorter and winter's nip is in the air, butchering day arrives. Meats are canned, smoked, or frozen for use throughout the cold months.

The Earth Grows Quiet

Winter is a time for repairs and maintenance around the farm. There are fewer demands from the fields and garden, so the farm family fix their energies on other projects. It is during these slower times when the earth is frozen and silent that many women turn to quiltmaking.

It would be misleading to say that all Amish women enjoy quilting. For some it is as natural as housecleaning and gardening. For others it is tedious work and something they simply prefer not to do. But for many women, it is a fulfilling undertaking learned at the elbows of their mothers and kept alive by tradition and their own enthusiasm.

Growing Up

Discipine is strict in Amish families and is evidenced in the children's ability to sit quietly during the three hour Sunday morning church services. Children are treated firmly but not harshly. They learn early to take responsibility around the farm and are often given specific chores in both house and farm work. One of the skills often taught young children is to handstitch small patches together for a quilt top. Not only do they learn a specific skill but these children are at the same time being taught perseverance, patience, and a lack of idleness. Young girls eventually learn to embroider and finally to make their own clothing. Along the way, most girls follow the example of the older women in their lives and also learn to quilt.

Families Wrapped in Love — and Quilts

Part of the magic of quilting is that it can be done in groups. Fun and visiting happen around the quilting frame. Young Amish women, like teenagers everywhere, dream about their futures. For most the choices are clearcut—marriage, family, and a carrying on of their way of life. It is not unusual for an Amish girl in her early teens to begin making several quilts in anticipation of her marriage and children.

Among the Amish, large families are received with great joy. And in preparation for these gifts from God, expectant mothers and grandmothers turn to making crib quilts. Most women are not employed outside of the home. They view mothering and caring for their homes as honorable and worthwhile positions. The responsibility of raising children in a God-fearing manner is foremost in the minds of these parents.

How do Amish women, with their large families and basic, back-to-earth lifestyle, find time to quilt? Time is a relative concept. Many Amish homesteads operate as extended families with two or three generations living under one roof. Although each family lives separately, there is daily interaction between generations. Consequently, both moral support and physical help flow in all directions. And children, although the primary care of their parents, relate closely to grandparents whose lifestyle and values match what they see at home.

Parents work hard at establishing "Amish" values in their offspring. However, as children become teenagers, they are gently freed of parental ties and the choice to leave or stay within the community is one that must be made by each individual. For many young adults marrying and joining the church happen at about the same time. Both are lifetime commitments supported by family and church.

The Amish are, in general, a restrained people. They show little overt emotion or affection. But in place of kisses and embraces, Amish women demonstrate their love through their offerings of quilts and favorite foods, both lovingly prepared and assembled. Many mothers make quilts to present to their sons and daughters at their marriages.

Some quilts seem to have been intended as heirlooms and show quilts, for use on beds only on Sundays and when company was coming. Both the memories of their owners and the condition of these bedcovers bear out this intent. These quilts are in such excellent condition that it seems they were never used. Perhaps the makers knew that the love invested in each tiny quilting stitch would serve as long time testament to that affection.

Quilting Belongs to All Ages

Growing old is not a tragedy in the Amish world. Age carries the respect of wisdom and the elderly are cared for

The Amish care for their own elderly instead of leaving that to Social Security. Additions are built onto the original farmhouse to make room for two or three generations.

with dignity. Aging family members are nursed at home unless they require hospitalization. Around the farm there are jobs that can keep men busy even though their strength and health may be failing. There is nearly always a son or grandson for them to assist.

Women stay involved in domestic chores and childcare until it becomes physically impossible for them. Here again quilting fits into the life cycle. Old age and new blood work elbow to elbow on a project that symbolizes Amish life. One generation learns from the next with the knowledge that time goes on and with it the cycle of life. Death is seen as a natural part of having lived. When one becomes old, death is the doorway to a new life and a stepping stone for the next generation.

Fan

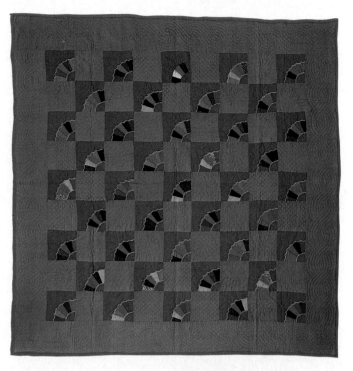

Fan, 1904. 79 x 80, Berks Co., Pennsylvania. Anna Lois Umble. One patch was done without the addition of embroidery around the fan.

A bright and cheerful quilt, the Fan is a pattern used largely by Amish women of the Midwest who borrowed it from their neighbors. But its organic quality makes it especially appropriate for these rural farm women. When fans are set in a quilt, all slanting in one direction, they resemble bright flowers leaning toward and drinking in the sunshine. When the blocks are tipped so that the fans stand upright they look like a mass of butterflies in flight. When patches are set opposite each other they remind one of the agitation of a butterchurn and when all four points are assembled together the fans form a wheel.

The Fan quilt may be a combination of piecing and appliquéing or it may be completely pieced. When the former method is used, the fans are first pieced, then appliquéd onto a background square. This means of construction is especially prevalent when the edge of the fan is scalloped.

Embroidery around the edges of the fans is an additional feature on some Amish Fan quilts. Quilting surrounds the fan design and decorates the borders.

New growth coming from the old is a universal theme. It is also found in the Amish community, both in nature and the church. The Fan pattern is reflected in the reel of this binder as it sheaves the wheat.

How To Make an Amish Quilt

Fan, dated 1927. Cotton, sateen, 76 x 85. Elkhart Co., Indiana. Diana Leone. Several pieces of black velvet add richness to this vibrant quilt.

How To Make an Amish Quilt

Fan

Approximate size 96 x 107

Measurements given <u>without</u> seam allowance

A — template given
B — template given
C — template given
D — width of border 15 inches

Make 42 pieced blocks

Assembly instructions:

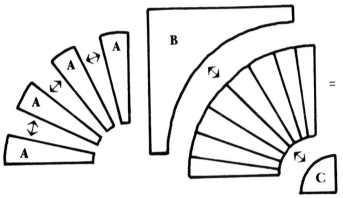

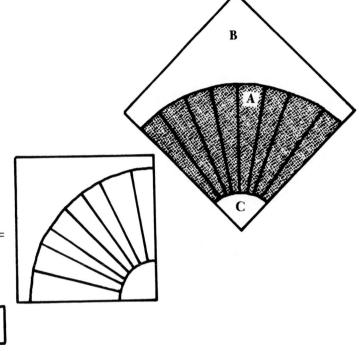

See Diagram 1, pg. 21 (Total Quilt Assembly).
See Border Application Diagram, pg. 23.

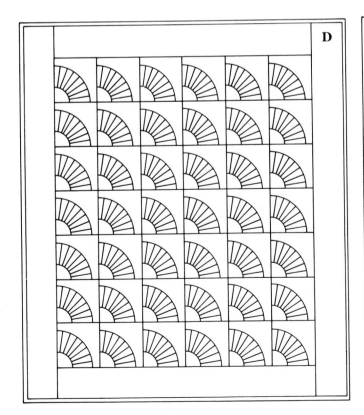

How To Make an Amish Quilt

How To Make an Amish Quilt

Fan
Approximate size 47 x 56

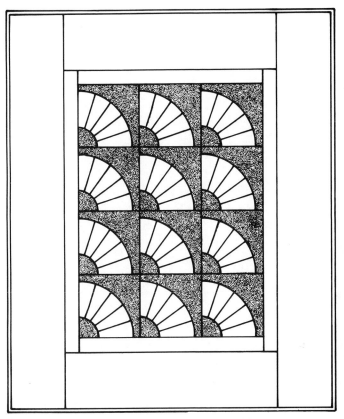

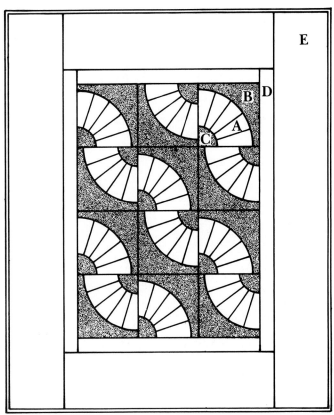

Measurements given <u>without</u> seam allowance

A — template given
B — template given
C — template given
D — width of inner border 2 inches
E — width of outer border 8 inches
Make 12 pieced blocks

Assembly instructions:

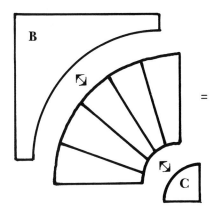

See Diagram 3, pg. 22 (Total Quilt Assembly).
See Border Application Diagram, pg. 23.

How To Make an Amish Quilt

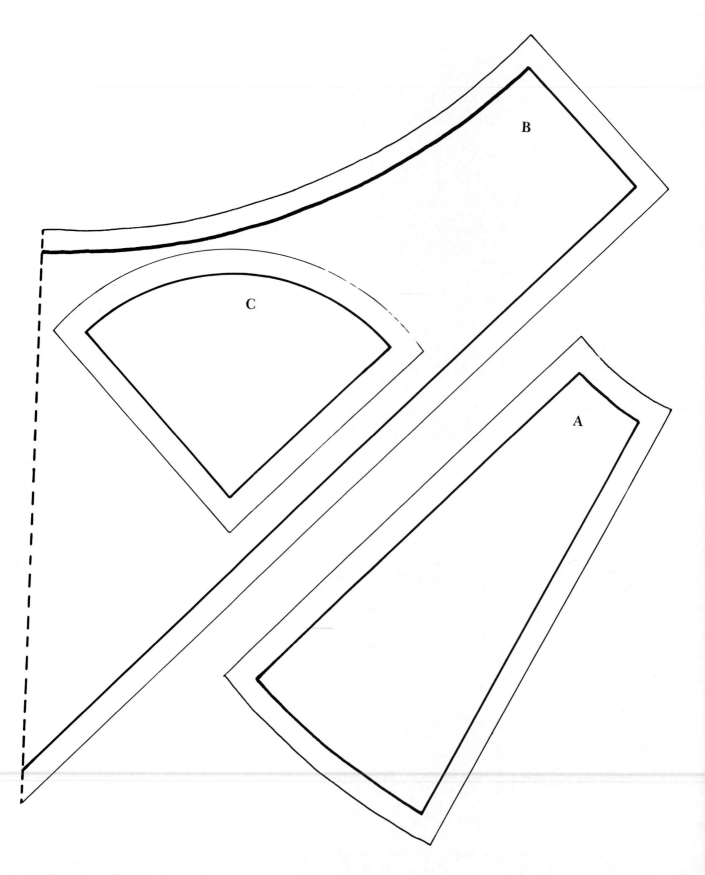

Ocean Waves

Ocean Waves is a pattern frequently seen in Midwestern Amish quilts but rarely used by the Pennsylvania Amish. The pattern exemplifies its name with small triangles creating movement and currents in the lines of the quilt.

Because of their limited travel and the landlocked locations of Amish settlements, the makers of these quilts likely never saw ocean waves. Despite that, the many variations of this pattern capture the mix of quiet and storm that bespeaks the ocean.

In general, Midwestern Amish quilters used brighter colors and more diverse patterns but paid less attention to the details of quilting than did Pennsylvania Amish quilters. In Ocean Waves the colors are generally quite bright. Yellow, a frequent choice for this pattern, appears less frequently among Pennsylvania Amish quilts but is common in the Midwest. As is typical of many Midwestern quilts, the borders and bindings of Ocean Waves are often narrower than on Pennsylvania quilts. Furthermore, instead of the elaborate feathered quilting often found on Pennsylvania borders, Midwestern quilting is often the more simple and easily executed cable design.

Ocean Waves, dated August 20, 1919. Cotton, 72 x 84. Holmes Co., Ohio. Judi Boisson Antique American Quilts, New York. The gray background seems to perk up the colors in the interior of the quilt.

The orange, slow-moving-vehicle symbols on the rear of these buggies look like the triangles on an Ocean Waves quilt. This hitching post has attracted a diversity of Amish buggies.

Ocean Waves, c. 1930. Cotton, 89 x 74. Holmes Co., Ohio. Judi Boisson Antique American Quilts, New York.

How To Make an Amish Quilt

Ocean Waves
Approximate size 96 x 108

Measurements given <u>without</u> seam allowance

A — template given
B — template given
C — Cut 9 triangles

8½ inches
8½ inches

D — Cut 2 triangles

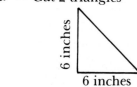

6 inches
6 inches

E — width of inner border 3 inches
F — width of outer border 9 inches

Make 15 pieced blocks
Make 11 half blocks
Make 2 quarter blocks

Darker line, below, indicates a single patch.

Assembly instructions:

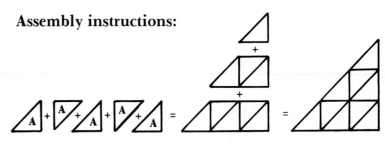

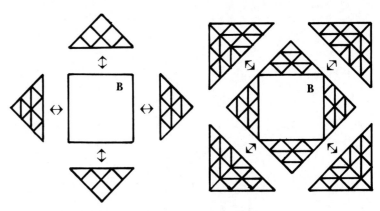

See Border Application Diagram, pg. 23.

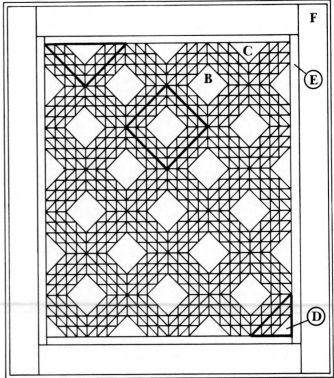

Variation 1

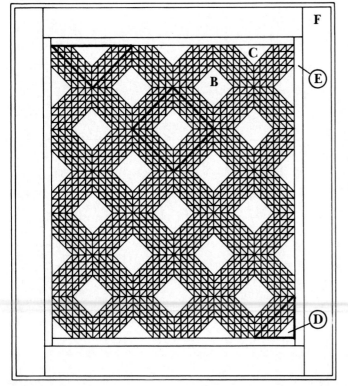

F
C
B
E
D

Variation 2

F
C
B
E
D

How To Make an Amish Quilt

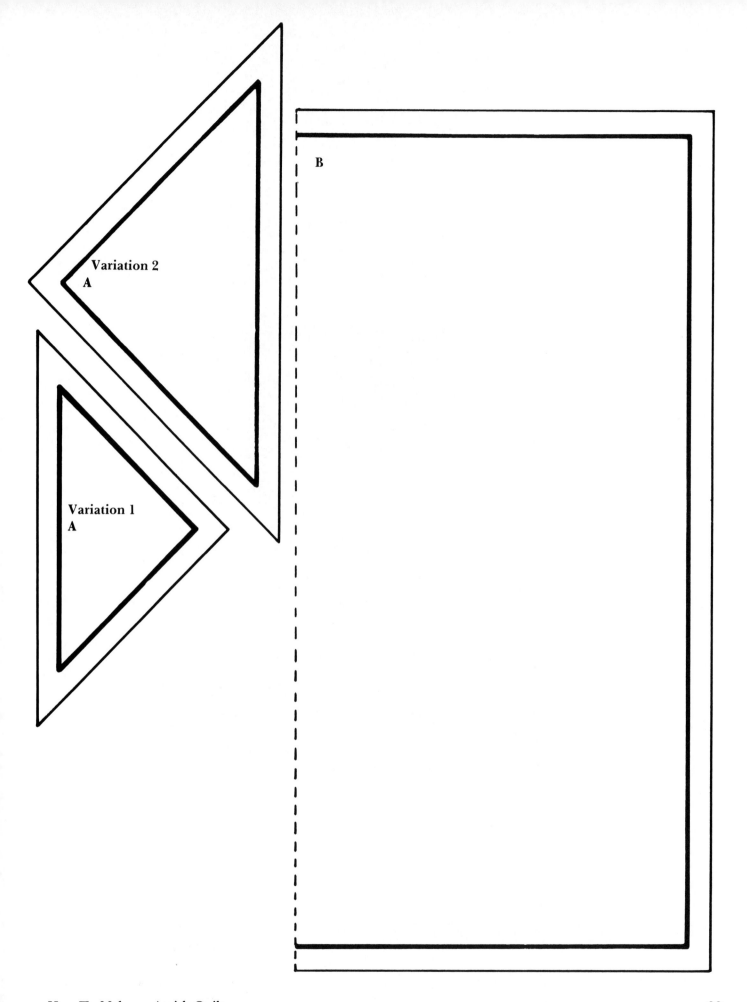

Variation 2
A

Variation 1
A

B

Ocean Waves
Approximate size 47 x 54

Measurements given <u>without</u> seam allowance

A — template given
B — template given
C — Cut 9 triangles

8½ inches
8½ inches

D — Cut 2 triangles

6 inches
6 inches

E — width of inner border 2 inches
F — width of outer border 8 inches

Make 15 pieced blocks   Make 11 half blocks

Make 2 quarter blocks

Assembly instructions:

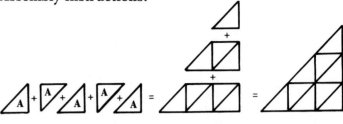

A + A + A + A + A =

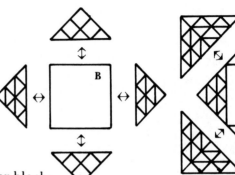

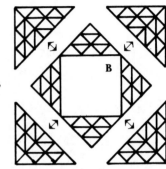

See Border Application Diagram, pg. 23.

B

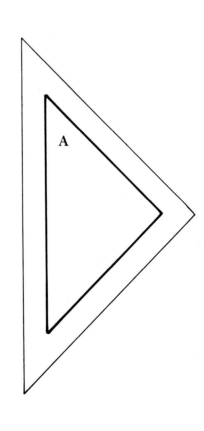

A

Roman Stripe

Roman Stripe is a pattern used mainly by Midwestern Amish quilters. A quilt of very simple construction, it may also be referred to as Shadows. In it, square blocks are equally divided with one half being a solid fabric and the other half being a series of diagonal strips ending with a triangle. The strips of brightly colored fabric are usually arranged in a random fashion. Although simply constructed, the overall effect of this pattern is an almost shocking burst of color and energy.

The arrangement of the quilt blocks can totally change the impact of the top. Blocks may be set in the quilt with each triangle pointing in the same direction. Another arrangement with the blocks put together in a zig-zag fashion creates the image of jagged streaks of lightning. And if the blocks are placed with four triangles coming together a diamond is formed. Many other possibilities exist and have been tried by the creative quilter.

Roman Stripe, dated 1934. Wool (small piece of velvet in center), 82 x 84. Topeka, LaGrange Co., Indiana. Rebecca Haarer. Use of a brown background makes this a quilt with a feeling of warmth, made by Susie Miller for her daughter as a wedding gift.

Sharp and easy angles of farm architecture could well be the inspiration for some quilt patterns. Parallel and alternating diagonal lines reflect both quilt lines and barn lines.

How To Make an Amish Quilt

Roman Stripe, dated 1906. Wool, 81 x 62. Holmes Co., Ohio. The Darwin D. Bearley Collection.

How To Make an Amish Quilt

Approximate size 96 x 106

Measurements given <u>without</u> seam allowance

A — template given
B — template given
C — template given
D — template given
E — template given
F — cut 42 triangles

10 inches
10 inches

G — width of inner border 3 inches
H — width of outer border 15 inches

Assembly instructions:

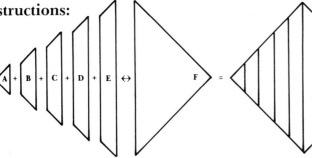

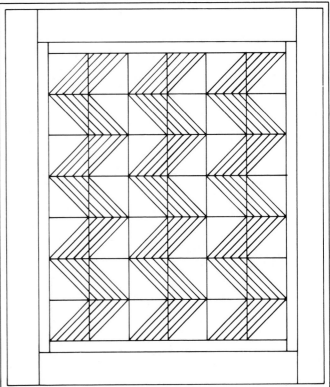

See Diagram 1, pg. 21 (Total Quilt Assembly).
See Border Application Diagram, pg. 23.

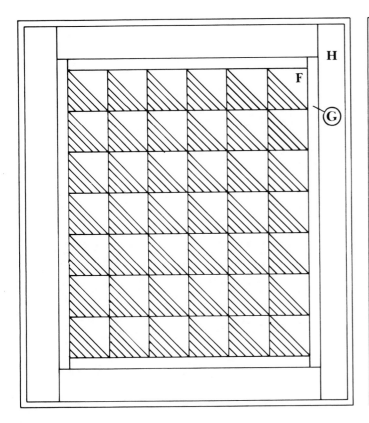

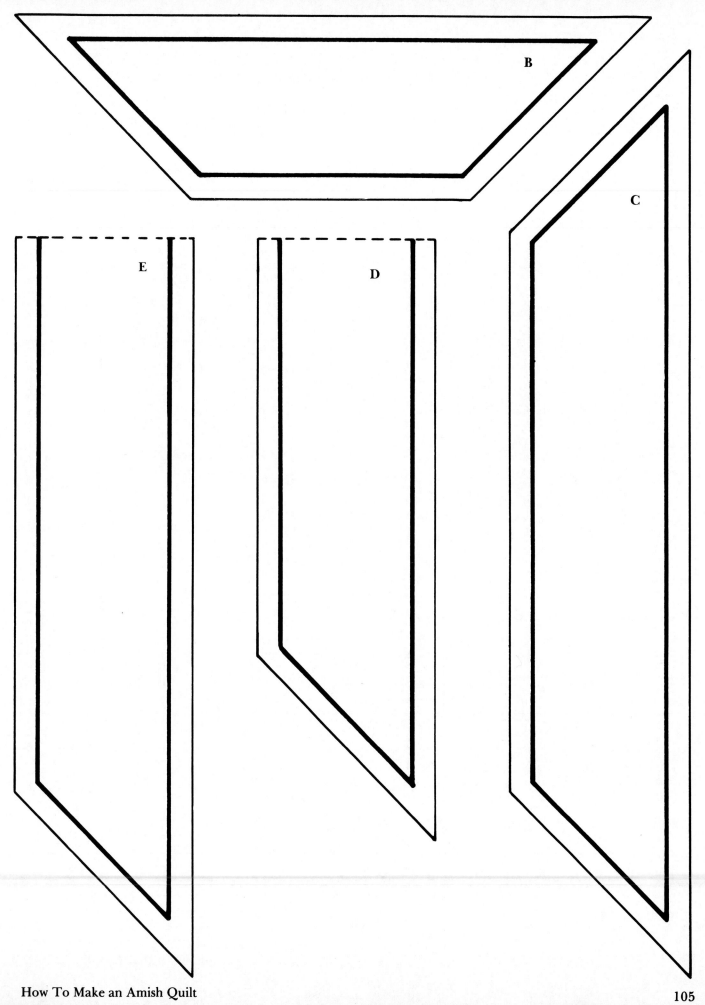

Roman Stripe
Approximate size 48 x 55

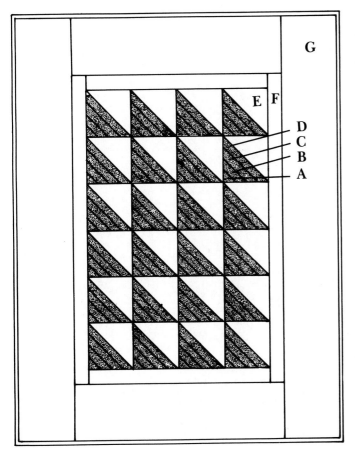

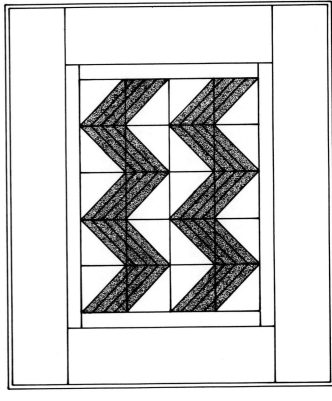

Assembly instructions:

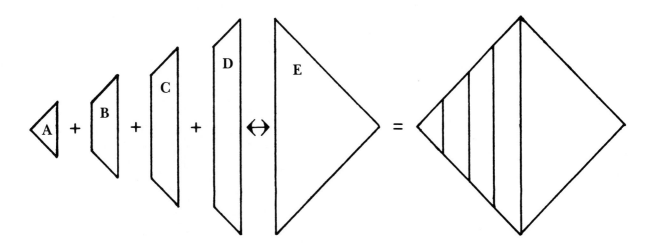

**See Diagram 3, pg. 22 (Total Quilt Assembly).
See Border Application Diagram, pg. 23.**

How To Make an Amish Quilt

Measurements given <u>without</u> seam allowance

A — template given
B — template given
C — template given
D — template given
E — cut 24 triangles

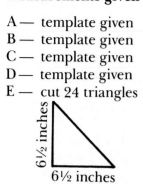

6½ inches

6½ inches

F — width of inner border 3 inches
G — width of outer border 8 inches

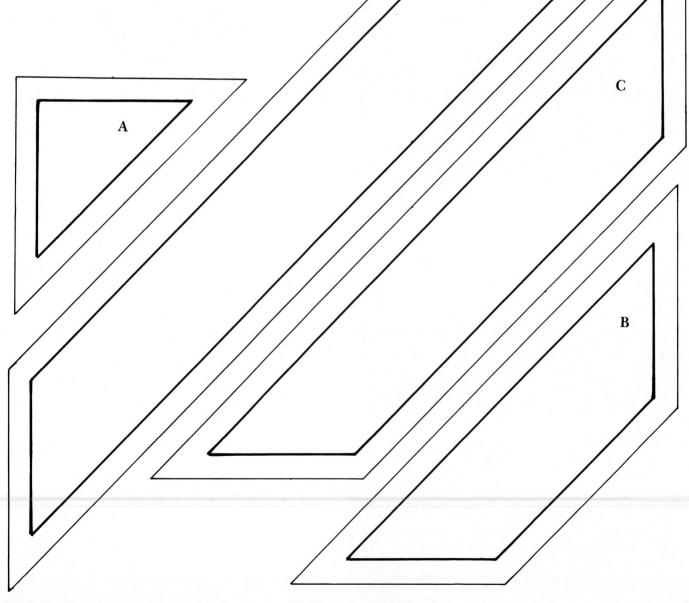

Tumbling Blocks

The Tumbling Blocks or Baby Blocks is a simple quilt but one with an intriguing interplay of color and apparent dimension. One can gaze at the Tumbling Block quilt for some time before all of its patterns emerge. By using a single diamond shape and the varied placement of colors, a quiltmaker can create an optical illusion of cubes, hexagons, stars, and diamonds. Occasionally the arrangement of colors also produces a large overall design on the quilt surface.

To achieve the illusion of stacked cubes one must have at least three fabrics in varying intensities of color—one dark, one medium, and one light. The diamonds must be arranged in a hexagon formation with the dark, medium, and light fabrics being used in the same positions throughout the quilt. If diamonds are simply arranged in a random fashion a star is likely to be the dominant emerging pattern.

Quilting stitches generally follow the outline of the diamonds on the pieced top. Surrounding borders are quilted in more fanciful designs.

Tumbling Blocks — Pyramid Variation, c. 1930-40. Cotton, rayon (worsted wool-cotton blend), 85 x 99. Ohio. Judi Boisson Antique American Quilts, New York. This is only a quilt top but shows a very successful achievement of a design within a pattern.

Families work together in all aspects of farm life. Here father and sons work beside each other loading straw, an image similar to Tumbling Blocks.

How To Make an Amish Quilt

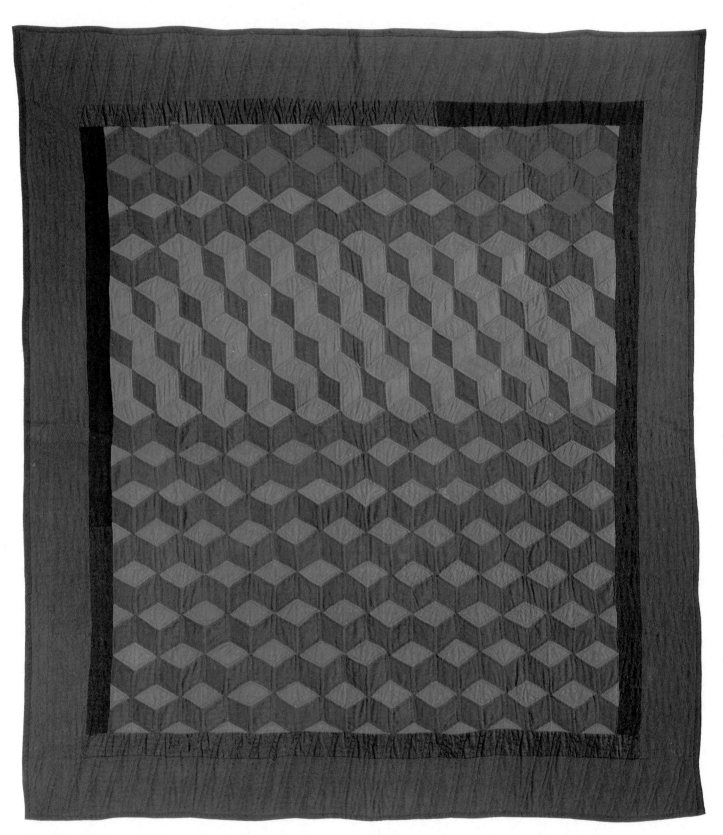

Tumbling Blocks, c. 1930. Cotton, 74 x 67. Ohio. Judi Boisson Antique American Quilts, New York. Well organized stacks of cubes form the body of this magnificent quilt.

How To Make an Amish Quilt

Tumbling Blocks
Approximate size 93 x 109

Measurements given <u>without</u> seam allowance
A — template given
B — template given
C — template given
D — width of inner border 3 inches
E — width of outer border 12 inches

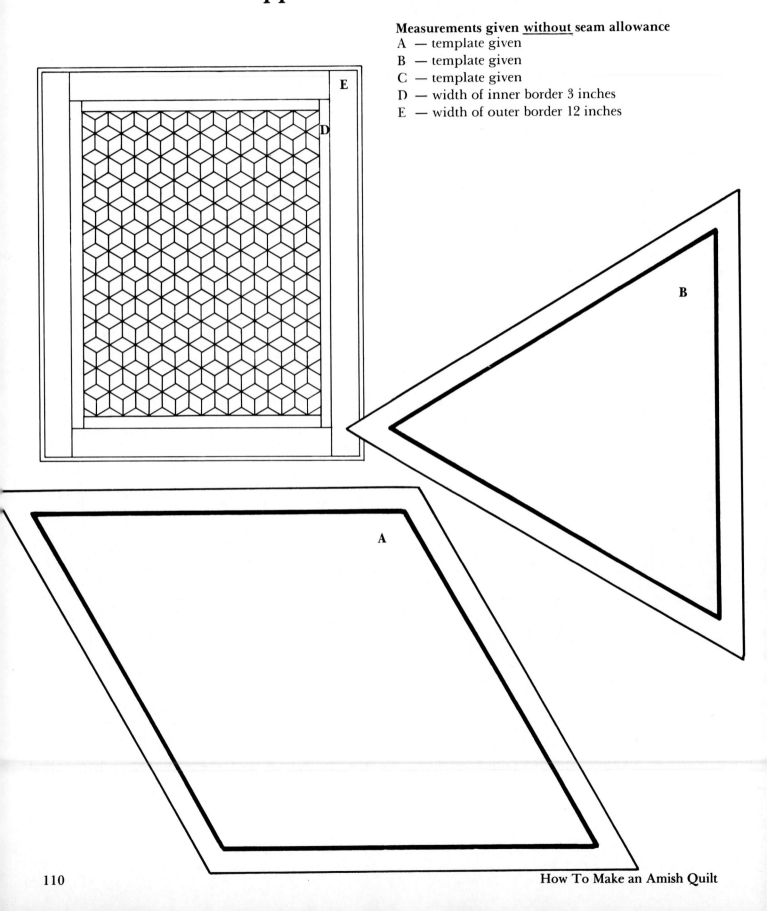

E

D

B

A

How To Make an Amish Quilt

Assembly instructions:

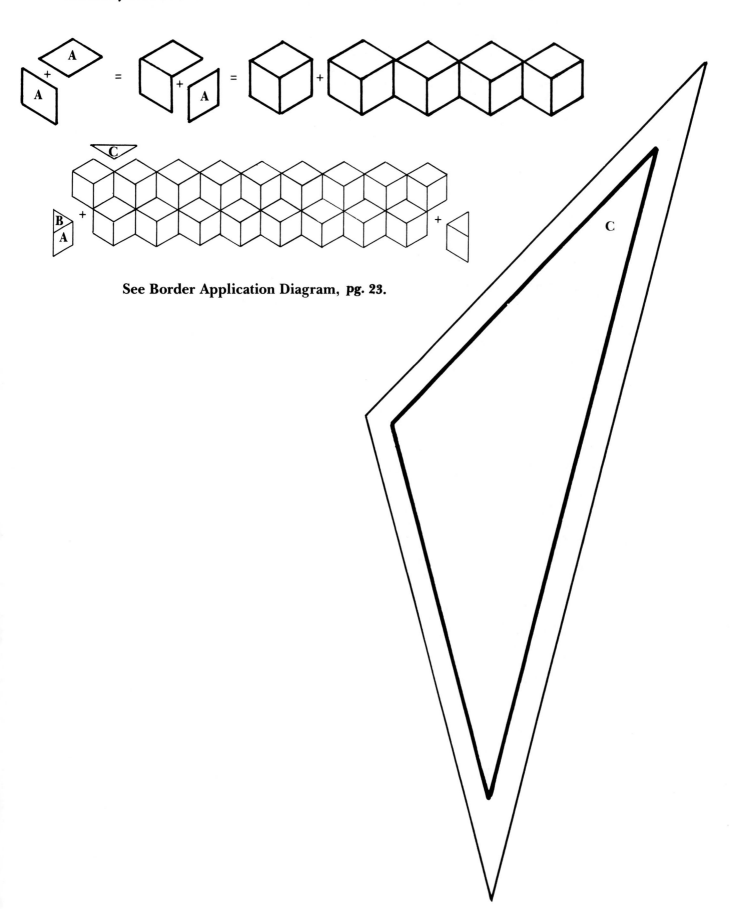

See Border Application Diagram, pg. 23.

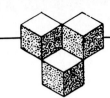

Tumbling Blocks
Approximate size 48 x 54

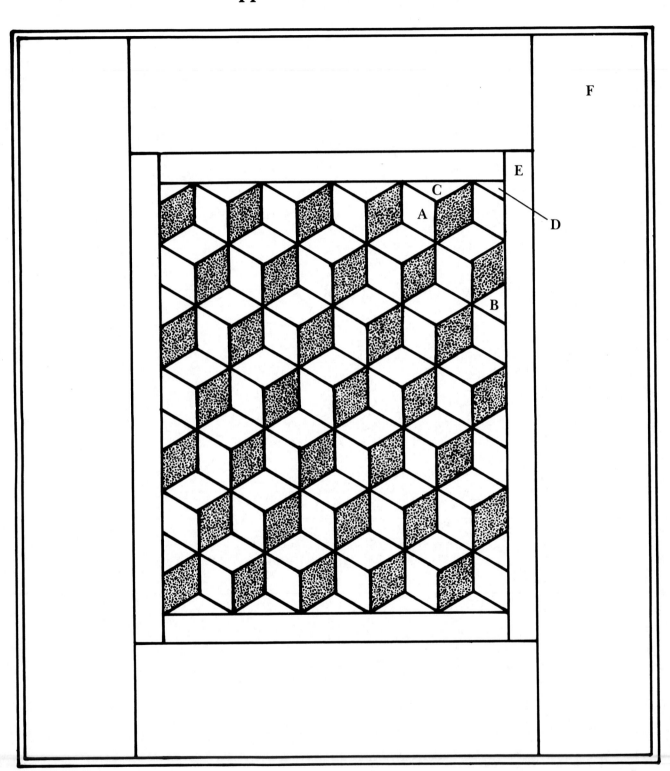

Measurements given <u>without</u> seam allowance

A — template given

B — template given

C — template given

D — width of inner border 2 inches

E — width of outer border 8 inches

How To Make an Amish Quilt

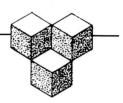

Assembly instructions:

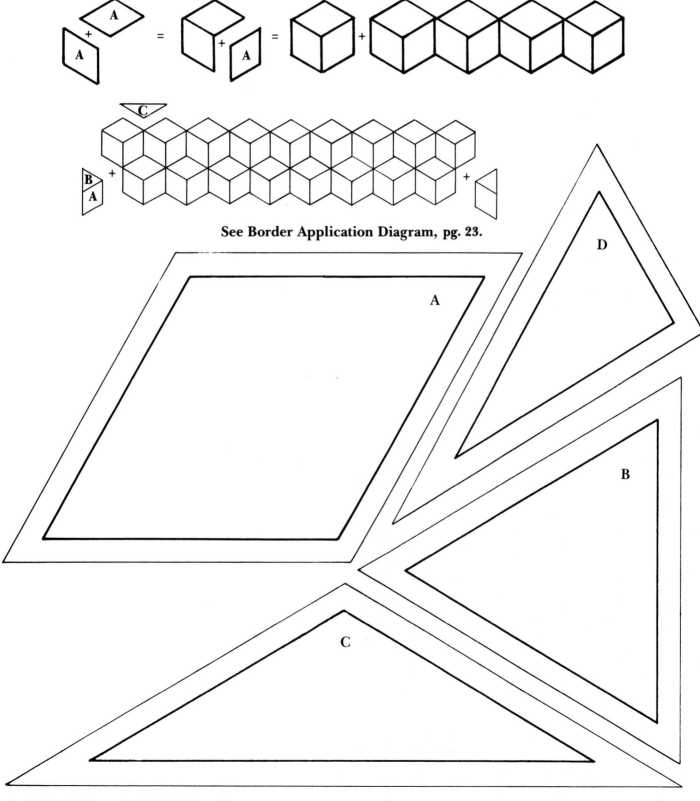

See Border Application Diagram, pg. 23.

Bow Tie

It is fascinating to observe that a group who chooses to avoid the wearing of men's ties makes the Bow Tie quilt pattern with such flair. Obviously there is much creative freedom permitted in quiltmaking. Although considered unnecessary and attention-getting as a clothing accessory, the bow tie as a design is not viewed as wrong if it is used within clear boundaries.

This is a delightful pattern with sprightly little bow ties nearly dancing across the quilt surface. Most often they are arranged in diagonal, vertical, or horizontal rows. On occasion they are set at angles to form a circle on the quilt top.

Possibly an alteration of the basic Four-Patch, the Bow Tie is much more difficult to construct because of the tiny square in the center of the tie. This requires that the four surrounding squares have one corner trimmed diagonally. When piecing, this angled corner must be set in against the bow tie, a task not easily achieved by beginners.

Quilting generally outlines the ties and becomes more plentiful on the one or more borders framing them.

Bow Tie Variation, c. 1900. Cotton, wool, 66 x 82. Loudenville, Ohio. Judi Boisson Antique American Quilts, New York. Bow ties are not as easily seen in this arrangement of the pattern.

Dress regulations within the various Amish groups are generally quite severe. Black outerwear is common. Black felt hats are worn by the men and boys in cold weather, straw hats in hot. Bow ties are only worn by Amish quilts, not Amish males.

114

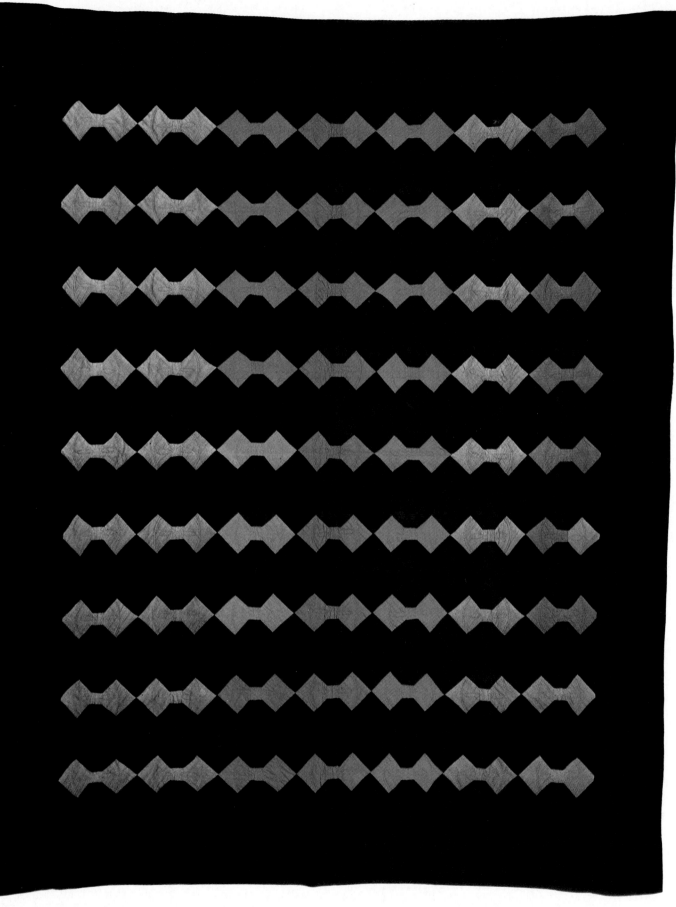

Bow Tie, dated 1919. Cotton, 70 x 84. Nappanee, Elkhart Co., Indiana. Rebecca Haarer. Set in straight horizontal rows, the ties seem to be arranged for some performance.

Bow Tie
Approximate size 95 x 108

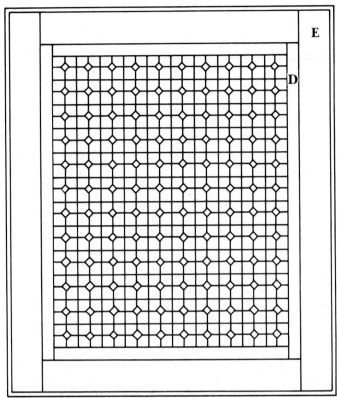

Variation 1

Measurements given <u>without</u> seam allowance

A — template given
B — template given
C — template given
D — width of inner border 3 inches
E — width of outer border 13 inches

Make 120 pieced blocks

Assembly instructions:

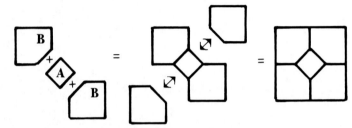

See Diagram 1, pg. 21 (Total Quilt Assembly).
See Border Application Diagram, pg. 23.

Variation 2

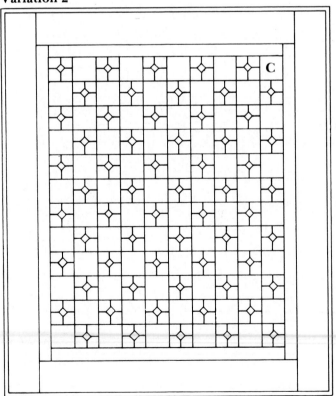

Variation 3

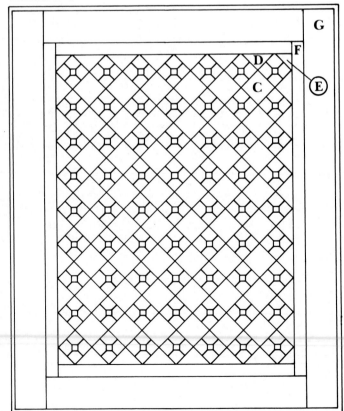

How To Make an Amish Quilt

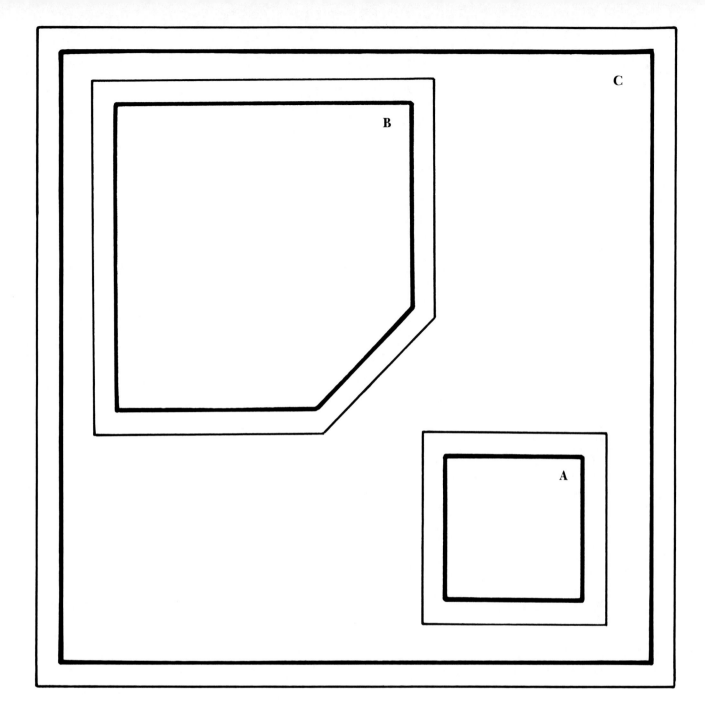

Variation 3

Measurements given <u>without</u> seam allowance

A — template given
B — template given
C — cut 48 squares template given
D — cut 28 triangles

6⅜ inches (vertical)
6⅜ inches (horizontal)

E — cut 4 triangles

4½ inches (vertical)
4½ inches (horizontal)

F — width of inner border 3 inches
G — width of outer border 13 inches

Make 63 pieced blocks

See Diagram 2, pg. 21 (Total Quilt Assembly).
See Border Application Diagram, pg. 23.

Bow Tie
Approximate size 45 x 55

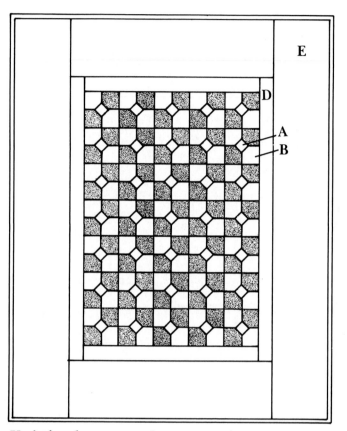

Variation 1

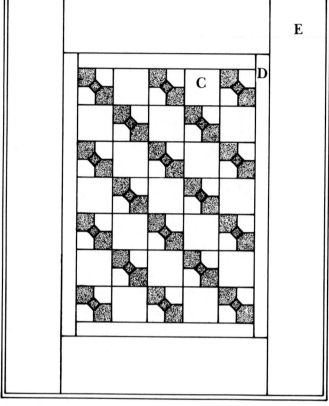

Variation 2

Measurements given <u>without</u> seam allowance

A — template given
B — template given
C — template given (used only for variations 2 and 3)
D — width of inner border 2 inches
E — width of outer border 8 inches
Make 35 pieced blocks (variation 2 make 12 pieced blocks)

Assembly instructions:

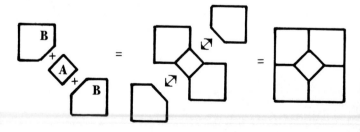

See Diagram 3, pg. 22 (Total Quilt Assembly).
See Border Application Diagram, pg. 23.

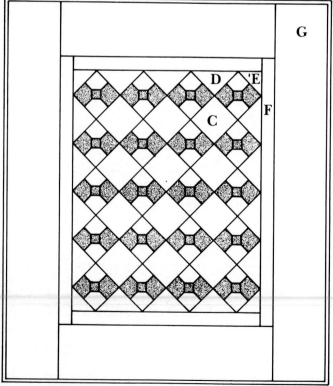

Variation 3

Variation 3
Measurements given <u>without</u> seam allowance

A — template given
B — template given
C — cut 12 squares template given
D — cut 14 triangles

5 inches / 5 inches

E — cut 4 triangles

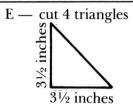

3½ inches / 3½ inches

F — width of inner border 2 inches
G — width of outer border 8 inches
Make 20 pieced blocks

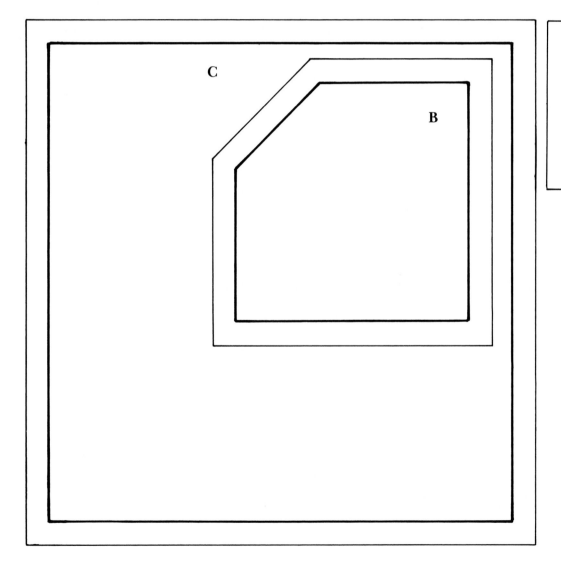

C

B

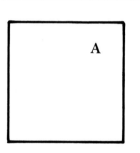

A

These Amish boys have congregated on the front porch of their school. The roof was on fire earlier in the day because the wood stove fire had gotten too hot.

Ice skating is a wonderful winter pasttime for many Amish. It's a time to let ice hockey and crack-the-whip add some zest to cold winter afternoons.

Excerpts from a Grandmother's Diary

This diary represents the life of an Amish woman throughout the year. Many of the entries were first published as news items in Amish publications. Names and places were changed to protect the identities of the people involved.

"Sadie's Diary" was originally compiled by the staff of The People's Place in Intercourse, Pennsylvania where it now hangs as a wall mural.

January 5 — Yesterday Amos Stoltzfus attended the funeral of Abner King of New York State. He died of a heart attack if he was informed right.

January 12 — I took in the quilting at the Ephrata Clothing Center.

January 21 — Martha wrote that they butchered a beef Tuesday.

January 24 — Snow piled high on the barnhill. The men had to shovel their way to get supplies.

February 2 — Sam Zooks had a singing on Sunday p.m. for the benefit of the visitors.

February 4 — Lizzie made fresh doughnuts all morning. She makes the best.

February 12 — Eli discouraged by hog prices.

February 15 — Cousin David A.'s had a get-together for some families who lost their children in accidents. Some came from as far as Indiana.

February 27 — Abe's crowd was here ice skating. They made hot dogs on the ice.

March 1 — Eli and Daudy were with a van load of Fisher relatives to Cumberland Co. to help build a hog barn at Joe's.

March 10 — This morning we had some excitement when I discovered a skunk in the cow barn!

March 14 — Yesterday was the sale of John F. Yoders. Lizzie and I helped with the chicken corn soup.

March 18 — Peas are finally in. An extra row this year.

March 26 — Children flying kites after school in the meadow these days.

April 4 — Aaron Jr. lost his best work horse. Somehow it must have stumbled down a bank in the cow lane and got under a barb wire fence and couldn't get up.

April 11 — We took supper with Bishop Junie Stoltzfuses after giving Jonas Fisher a surprise visit in the p.m.

April 17 — Plowing going good. Neighbor with tractor says it's too wet to get in the fields but our men having no problems.

April 25 — The boys hauled the grill out of the washhouse and we had grilled sausage for supper. Was a bit nippy to eat outside.

May 7 — Rachel came to help with planting the flower garden. Her new bread recipe hits the spot!

May 13 — Fresh asparagus, new rhubarb with tapioca and oranges, and the last of the roosters.

May 14 — The corn's in! The men worked from dawn till dark for five days. Amos and Elam took turns staying home from school.

May 29 — School picnic. Lizzie says several families from Honey Brook moving to Missouri. Joe Esh's might be going.

May 30 — Rain would be appreciated.

June 1 — I'm trying not to eat too many strawberries. They have too much acid for my arthritis.

June 14 — We did up 109 quarts of peas. Daudys helped.

June 20 — Eli and Abe went to the liability meeting at Christ Millers in Mary County, MD.

June 29 — Weather warm and humid again. Where did spring go? Warm weather is hard on J. J. Miller's Johnny with his condition.

July 3 — Yesterday afternoon lightning struck close and knocked Jonas A. Smucker down but he got up by himself, and 2 of Jake B's girls were in the cellar and it gave them a hard jolt.

July 14 — Black raspberries are at an end; sweet corn is on the menu, string beans are plentiful, also weeds in spite of the dry weather.

July 23 — Wheat is cut and is on shock. Some farmers started to thrash.

July 30 — The 21 qts. apricots we canned from the neighbor's tree will save us some peach canning.

August 7 — Clover got washed again today. Has been hard to put up hay at times.

August 14 — The last two days were spent in painting the school house inside and out, except the stucco. Had a few extra men at the table.

August 21 — Did up tomato juice today with Lizzie. 56 quarts!

August 22 — Surprise visit from O'Brien family from New Jersey. Learned to know them last summer at Junie's.

September 8 — Church services today were held in shed at Sammy Riehls with a large attendance.

September 16 — Mrs. James B. Hamilton, my roommate when I was in hospital, here for supper tonight. Her husband died in November.

September 19 — Leaves turning yellow in orchard. First frost last night.

September 27 — There was a bad accident last evening around 10. A car without lights on the wrong side of the road drove head-on into Levi Kauffman's horse, killing it almost instantly. It threw Levi about 20 feet across the car, breaking his pelvis.

October 4 — Today a pair of dark frame plastic glasses with bifocals were found along Railroad Ave. in a black case.

October 12 — John Lapps had a circle letter get-together last week after the meeting.

October 18 — Eli and the boys working late on the corn. Eli's back tired again.

October 23 — Helped make snitz pie for church at Aaron Jr's Sunday.

October 29 — Small game season opened today. What a racket!

November 1 — On Halloween morn a farm hand came to stay with Aaron Jr's., missing his sister Rebecca's birthday by 39 minutes. He will answer to the name of Jacob, named after Lizzie's father.

November 3 — Laura Petersheim had a quilting today to give to our teacher (non-Amish).

November 12 — Today was the wedding at Eli B. Fishers of their oldest daughter Barbara to Samuel E. Zook, son of Pre. Dan Zook. Several hundred ate at dinner, even more for supper.

November 22 — Another wedding, our sixth this month. Cousin Junie Beiler's Sarah hitched to a Larry Bontrager from Ohio. They met when Sarah went to help her aunt last year.

December 7 — Little Lydia Smoker is sick with fever and earache so she can't go to school.

December 17 — Daudy's are going along to the school program. Children working hard on memorization. It tickles me the way Amos is determined.

December 24 — It's snowing tonight, really coming down. Looks like we'll have a white Christmas.

December 26 — Second Christmas. Joes came over on the sleigh and Lizzie helped me with the meal. Duck and oyster filling. Cookies galore. A happy time for all.

December 31 — Another year. "Are we thankful enough the way we have it?"

How To Make an Amish Quilt

As the year goes round so do the seasons. Amish farmers are able to begin plowing earlier in the spring than their tractor-driving neighbors. Because horses are lighter in weight than tractors, they can enter the fields before it is as dry as a tractor requires.

Cultivating corn is a precise job but one often given to young children since it does not require exceptional strength.

Corn binders cut stalks of corn off at ground level and tie them in bundles. These loads of corn are then chopped and put into silos for the livestock throughout the winter. When the silos are filled, the corn is left to dry. Shell corn is then ground and mixed into short feed for cows.

Robbing Peter to Pay Paul

This pattern, known to quilters in general, was likely borrowed by an Amish woman from a non-Amish quilter friend. The quilt is often done in only two colors which enhances the power of the finished design.

Robbing Peter to Pay Paul is a logical label for this design: a section of one patch is robbed to fill a gap in the next. The positive and negative aspect of this pattern creates a sharp, clear circular design on the quilt top.

Curved lines make this a pattern for a quilter with experience since a pieced pattern with curved lines increases the potential for puckers and buckles. Curved edges must be very accurately cut and sewn to achieve a smooth, flat finish.

Quilting designs are stitched on the borders and in the larger patch between circles. Other pieced sections are simply outlined with quilting.

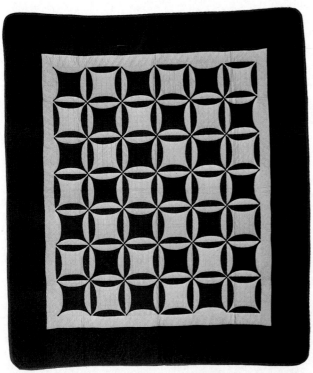

Robbing Peter to Pay Paul, 1905-10. Cotton, 68 x 74. Nappanee, Elkhart Co., Indiana. Rebecca Haarer. Light and dark fabrics provide excellent contrast for this pattern of positive and negative space.

Robbing Peter to Pay Paul, c. 1910-15. Cotton, 82 x 66. LaGrange Co., Indiana. Joseph M. B. Sarah. The smooth lines of this curved pattern must have been crafted by a master quiltmaker.

How To Make an Amish Quilt

Robbing Peter to Pay Paul
Approximate size 96 x 106

Measurements given <u>without</u> seam allowance

A — template given

B — template given

C — width of inner border 3 inches

D — width of outer border 10 inches

Make 56 pieced blocks

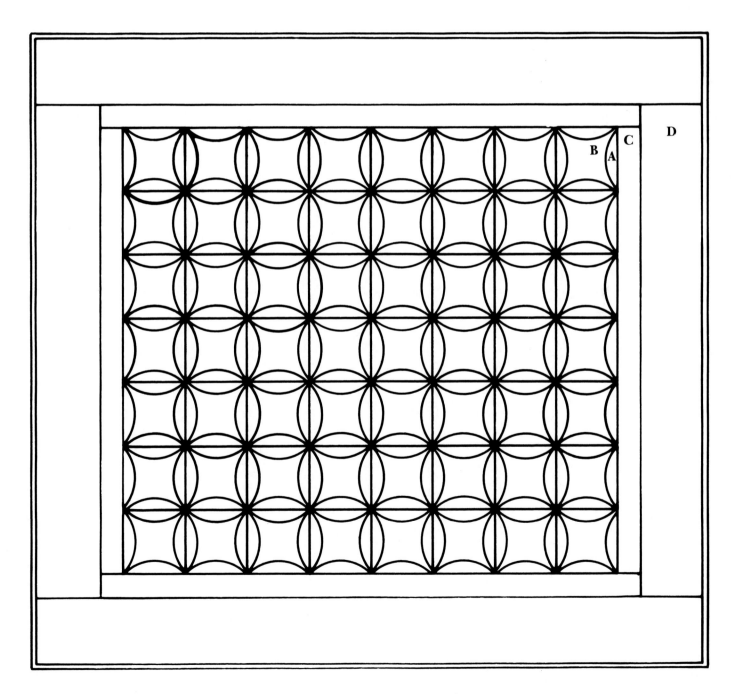

Assembly instructions:

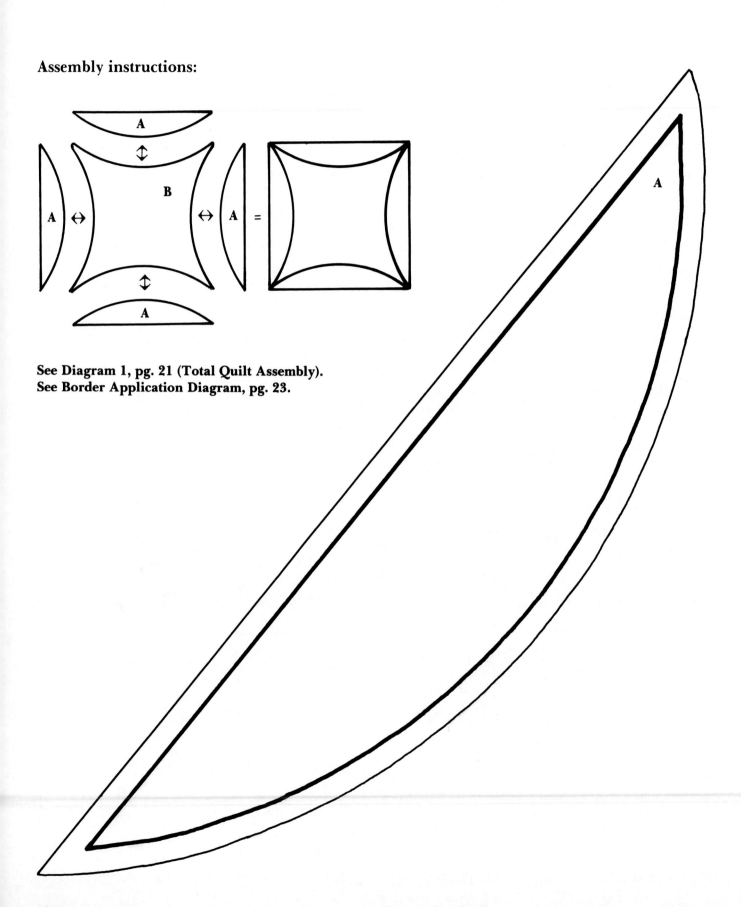

See Diagram 1, pg. 21 (Total Quilt Assembly).
See Border Application Diagram, pg. 23.

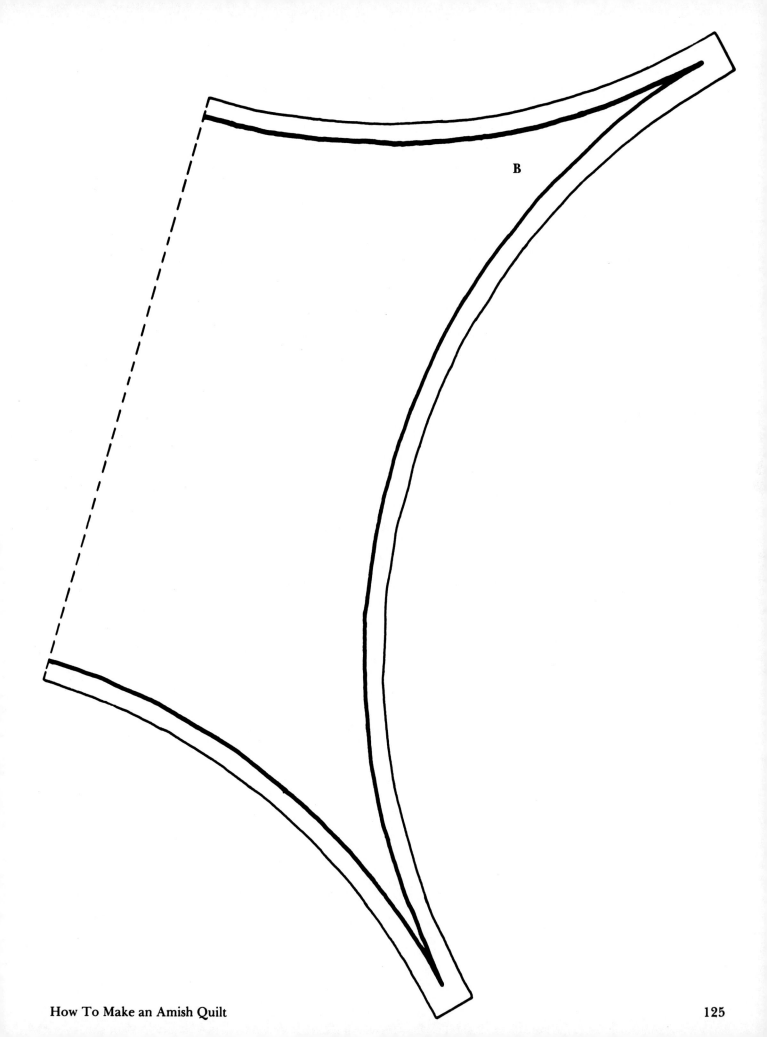

B

Robbing Peter to Pay Paul
Approximate size 48 x 55

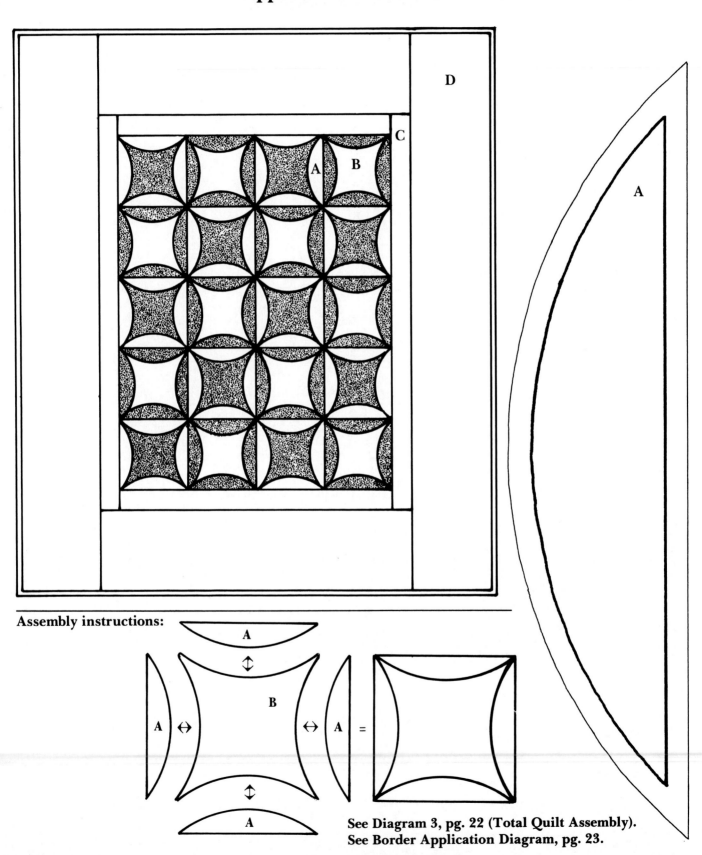

Assembly instructions:

See Diagram 3, pg. 22 (Total Quilt Assembly).
See Border Application Diagram, pg. 23.

How To Make an Amish Quilt

Measurements given <u>without</u> seam allowance

A — template given
B — template given
C — width of inner border 2 inches
D — width of outer border 8 inches
Make 20 pieced blocks

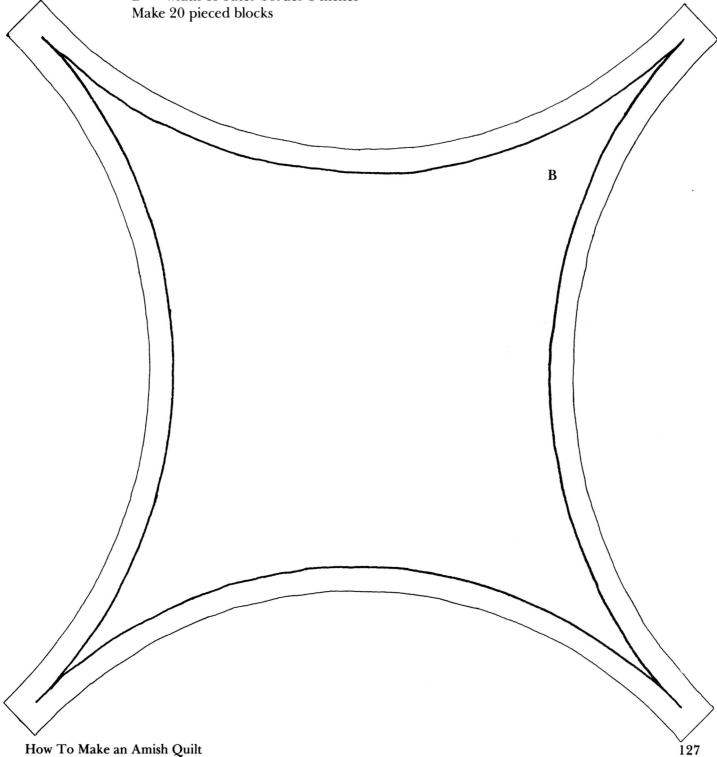

B

Shoo-fly

Shoo-fly Variation, dated January 9, 1913. Cotton, 72 x 84. LaGrange Co., Indiana. Rebecca Haarer.

Shoo-fly, c. 1925. Wool, cotton sateen, 68 x 72. Mifflin Co., Pennsylvania. William B. Wigton. Quilted cloverleafs fill alternate plain patches and hearts cover the inner border on this bedcover.

A visitor to an Amish home need not be there long to discover the outstanding culinary skills of these plain people. Their food is basic, plentiful and, for the most part, homegrown. Since the Amish remain largely an agrarian, hardworking people, foods·tend to be heavier and richer than many more sedentary urban- and suburbanites can handle. Cream, butter, eggs, meat, vegetables, and even fruit are readily accessible on many farms. They are therefore used in cooking, creating a delightful spread on the farm kitchen table.

One of the well-known pies associated with the Amish is shoo-fly pie. It is a sweet rich dessert with a gooey molasses bottom topped with spicy cake and baked in a flaky pie crust. Because the pie is so sweet it is said to have attracted flies during the baking process. Hence the name shoo-fly.

Since the Amish are well-known for both delights it seems appropriate that a quilt should bear the name of this notorious dessert, although no visual connection is apparent. The block is a basic nine-patch with some of the blocks halved to create triangles. The same pattern is also known as a Fence Row by some quilters. Patches are generally framed with one or more borders providing plenty of space for the skilled quilter.

How To Make an Amish Quilt

Fence Row, 1908. Cotton, 84 x 72. Nappanee, Elkhart Co., Indiana. Rebecca Haarer. Background fabric is pieced and varies slightly in shade but it only seems to add to the overall beauty of the quilt.

How To Make an Amish Quilt

Shoo-fly
Approximate size 90 x 104

Measurements given <u>without</u> seam allowance

A — template given
B — template given
C — cut 12 squares 10½ inches by 10½ inches
D — cut 14 triangles

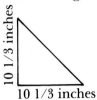

10 1/3 inches (vertical)
10 1/3 inches (horizontal)

E — cut 4 triangles

7½ inches (vertical)
7½ inches (horizontal)

F — width of inner border 3 inches
G — width of outer border 12 inches

Make 20 pieced blocks

Assembly instructions:

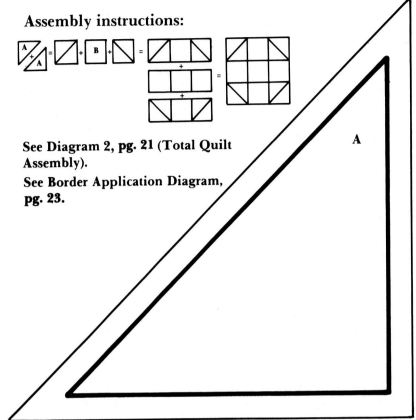

See Diagram 2, pg. 21 (Total Quilt Assembly).
See Border Application Diagram, pg. 23.

A

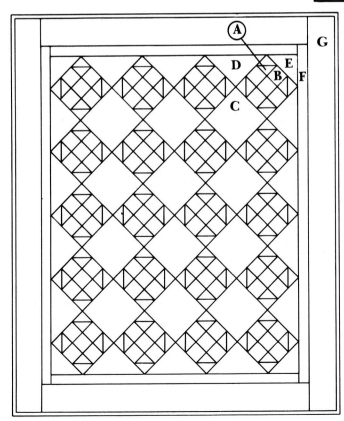

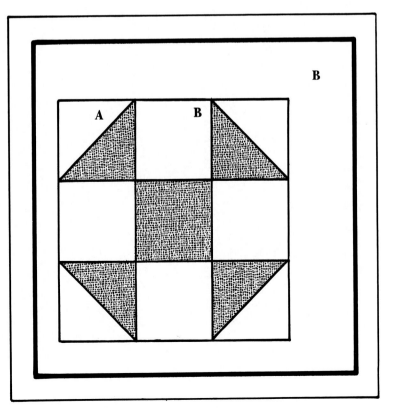

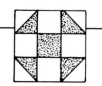

Shoo-Fly
Approximate size 46 x 58

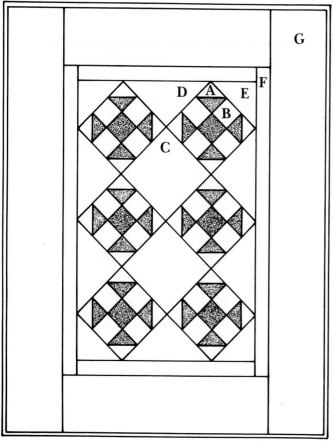

Measurements given <u>without</u> seam allowance

A — template given
B — template given
C — cut 2 squares 9 inches by 9 inches
D — cut 6 triangles

E — cut 4 triangles

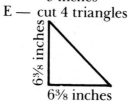

F — width of inner border 2 inches
G — width of outer border 8 inches
Make 6 pieced blocks

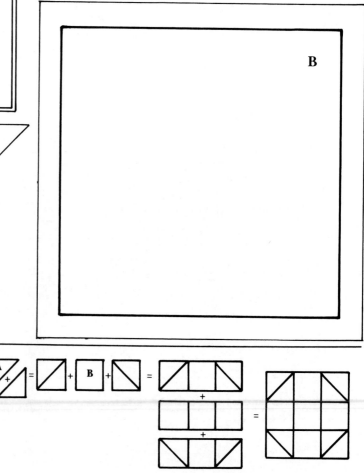

Assembly instructions:

See Diagram 4, pg. 22. (Total Quilt Assembly).   See Border Application Diagram, pg. 23.

How To Make an Amish Quilt

Monkey Wrench

Monkey Wrench, c. 1924. Cotton, 83 x 69. Elkhart Co., Indiana. Rebecca Haarer.

Another name for the Monkey Wrench design is Hole in the Barn Door. Both are apt descriptions for the pattern created by this combination of geometric shapes.

There are not sharp lines drawn between domestic tasks and farm tasks in an Amish home. Women are generally aware of and part of decisions made concerning the farm operations. Nor is it unusual to see women helping in the fields, milking cows, and tending chickens.

Perhaps this quilt pattern is a statement of the overlap in domestic chores, farm work, and the often more pleasurable task of quiltmaking. The monkey wrench (pipe wrench) is a tool found on any farm. One never knows when an implement will need minor repairs during planting or harvest season. And perhaps the Hole in the Barn Door label was inspired by an imaginative woman who saw the possibility of a quilt pattern in the cut-out of the stable door, designed to provide ventilation for farm animals.

The design is achieved through use of triangles and squares or rectangles to form a square patch. These patches may be set straight or tipped on an angle in the quilt top. When set on an angle, the blocks are set alternately with solid squares of fabric which lend themselves well to a fancy quilting design. The blocks are usually framed by one or more borders filled with flowing quilting.

The Monkey Wrench quilt is also called Hole in the Barn Door. Is there any question about why?!

How To Make an Amish Quilt

Monkey Wrench, 1911. Cotton, 82 x 72. LaGrange Co., Indiana. Rebecca Haarer. Blocks have been pieced and arranged in symmetry throughout this quilt.

How To Make an Amish Quilt

Monkey Wrench
Approximate size 88 x 102

Variation 1

Measurements given without seam allowance
A — template given
B — template given
C — width of sashing 4¼ inches
D — width of border 12 inches

Make 20 pieced blocks

Assembly instructions:

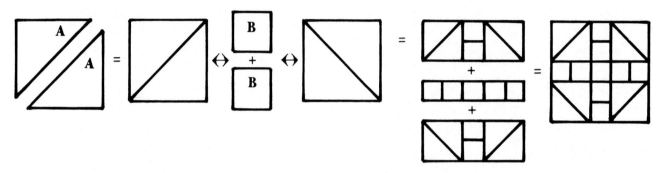

See Diagram 1, pg. 21 (Total Quilt Assembly).
See Border Application Diagram, pg. 23.

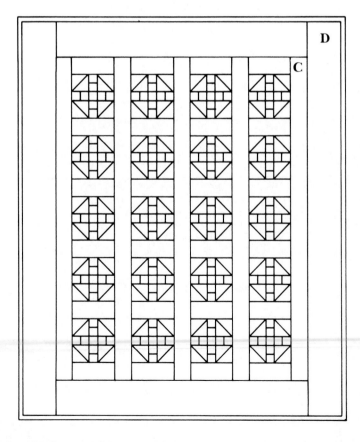

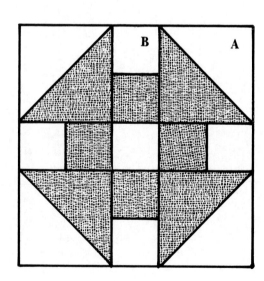

How To Make an Amish Quilt

Variation 2

Measurements given <u>without</u> seam allowance

A — template given
B — template given
C — cut 12 squares 10½ inches
D — cut 14 triangles

10½ inches · 10½ inches

E — cut 4 triangles

7½ inches · 7½ inches

F — width of border 15 inches

Make 20 pieced blocks

See Diagram 2, pg. 21 (Total Quilt Assembly).
See Border Application Diagram, pg. 23.

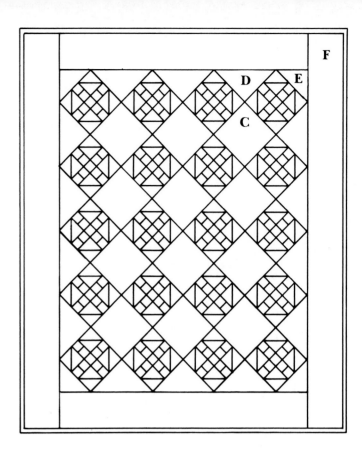

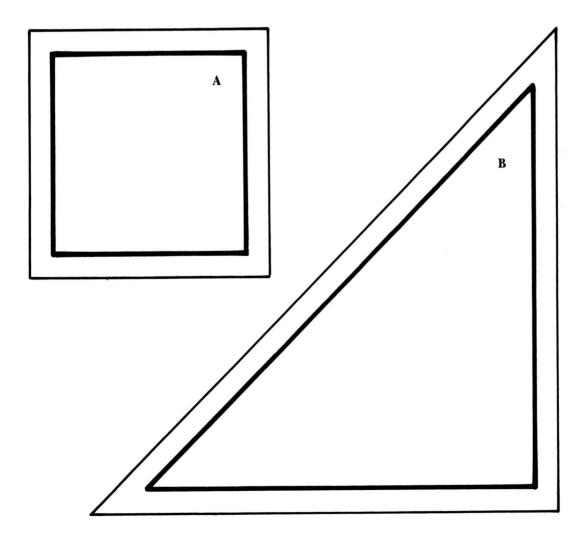

Monkey Wrench
Approximate size 46 x 57

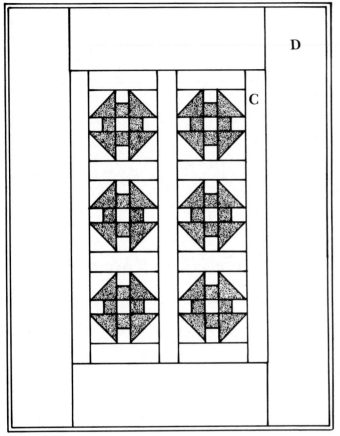

Variation 1

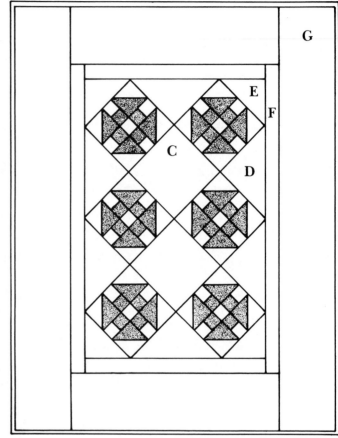

Variation 2

Measurements given <u>without</u> seam allowance

A — template given
B — template given
C — width of sashing and inner border 2½ inches
D — width of border 8 inches
Make 6 pieced blocks

Assembly instructions:

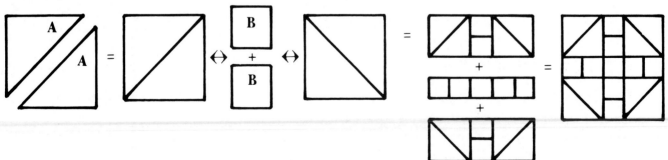

See Diagram 3, pg. 22 (Total Quilt Assembly).
See Border Application Diagram, pg. 23.

How To Make an Amish Quilt

Variation 2
Approximate size 46x58
Measurements given <u>without</u> seam allowance

A — template given
B — template given
C — cut 2-9 inch squares
D — cut 6 triangles

9 inches | 9 inches

E — cut 4 triangles

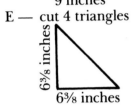

6⅜ inches | 6⅜ inches

F—width of inner border 2 inches
G—width of outer border 8 inches

Make 6 pieced blocks

See Diagram 4, pg. 22 (Total Quilt Assembly).
See Border Application Diagram, pg. 23.

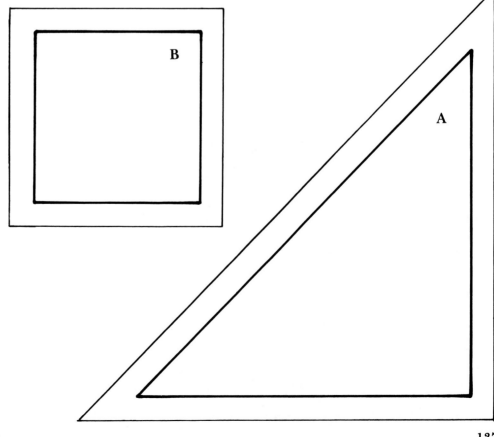

Carolina Lily

North Carolina Lily, c. 1920-30. Cotton, 75 x 77. Holmes Co., Ohio. The Darwin D. Bearley Collection. Pattern, colors, borders, binding, and quilting make this a real showpiece.

It is rare to find the Carolina Lily pattern among Amish quilts. And yet, its occasional presence indicates that a few Amish women were captivated by its beauty and did create quilts of this design.

The Amish have a high respect for nature and its gifts. Living close to the soil makes them more conscious of the earth's bounty and beauty. But because the Amish take seriously the Old Testament commandment against making graven images, they have traditionally kept from reproducing realistic images from nature. But, as in all of life, there are exceptions. And so occasionally, the Carolina Lily image appears.

The lilies and baskets of this pattern are pieced triangles, squares, and rectangles. Stems and handles are appliqued, a technique seldom used in antique Amish quilts.

This is a showy pattern and if a quiltmaker went to the trouble of piecing it, she was likely to cover it with extravagant quilting designs. There is ample space between flower baskets and on borders to absorb this exuberant work.

Carolina Lily, 1883-93. Cotton, 76 x 76. Davidsville, Somerset Co., Pennsylvania. Romaine S. Sala. The papers hand-stitched on the corners of this quilt read as follows: "Romaine's quilt pieced and quilted by G Pa Kaufmans Mother Christian Johns Kaufman" and "This is Nora's quilt."

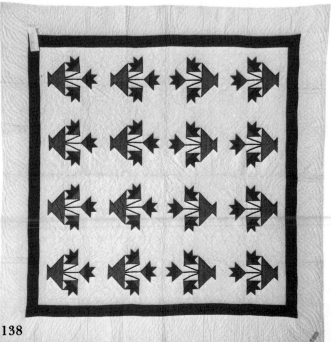

How To Make an Amish Quilt

Carolina Lily
Approximate size 90 x 104

Measurements given <u>without</u> seam allowance

A — template given
B — template given
C — template given
D — template given
E — template given
F — template given
G — template given
H — template given
I — template given
J — template given
K — template given
L — cut 12 squares 10½ x 10½ inches

M — cut 14 triangles

10½ inches / 10½ inches

N — cut 4 triangles

7½ inches / 7½ inches

O — width of inner border 3 inches
P — width of outer border 12 inches

Make 20 pieced blocks

Assembly instructions:

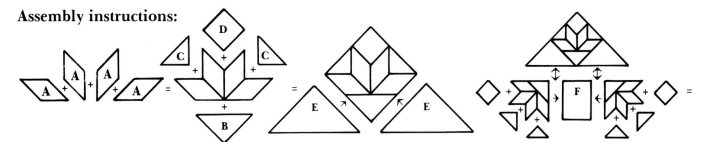

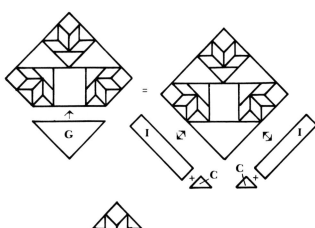

See Diagram 2, pg. 21 (Total Quilt Assembly).
See Border Application Diagram, pg. 23.

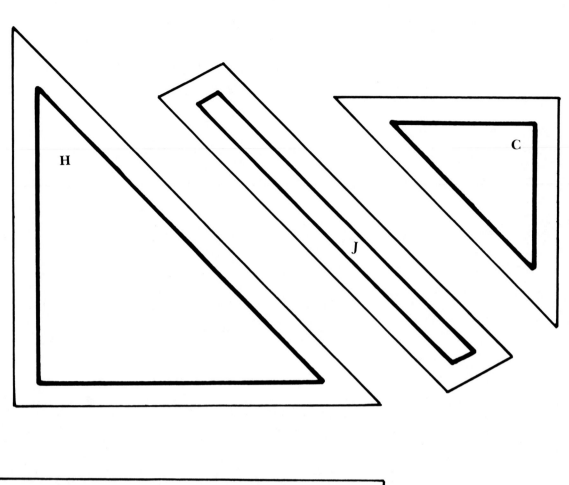

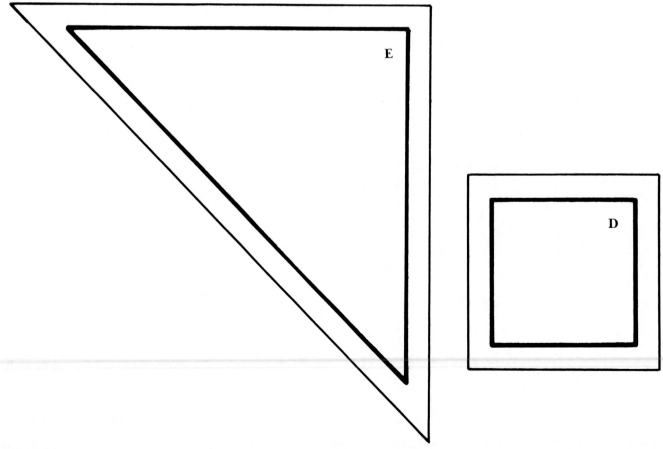

How To Make an Amish Quilt

Carolina Lily
Approximate size 46 x 58

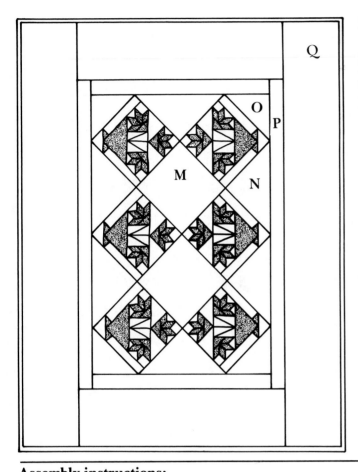

Measurements given <u>without</u> seam allowance

A — template given   G — template given
B — template given   H — template given
C — template given   I — template given
D — template given   J — template given
E — template given   K — template given
F — template given   L — template given

M— cut 2 squares 9 inches by 9 inches
N— cut 6 triangles

9 inches / 9 inches

O — cut 4 triangles

6⅜ inches / 6⅜ inches

P — width of inner border 2 inches
Q— width of outer border 8 inches
Make 6 pieced blocks

Assembly instructions:

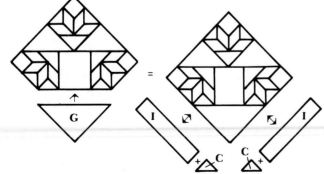

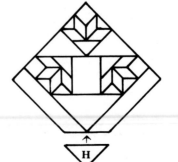

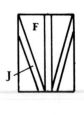

See Diagram 4, pg. 22 (Total Quilt Assembly).
See Border Application Diagram, pg. 23.

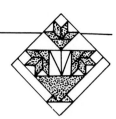

A

E

B

J

G

H

C

F

K

D

I

L

Crown of Thorns

Crown of Thorns, c. 1920. Cotton, 76 x 88. Collected LaGrange Co., Indiana. Rebecca Haarer.

Some quilt patterns are possibly taken from biblical themes. This single row of corn stalks also reminds one of the Crown of Thorns motif.

The Amish are a people deeply committed to God. However, most of these groups are not openly expressive about their faith. In general, Old Order groups do not proselytize. The groups are growing in number mostly because of their large families. It is significant that a high percentage of young people choose to join and remain in the Amish church.

Crown of Thorns is one of the few Amish quilts with distinctively religious connections. It directs one's thinking to the Passion and suffering of Christ. The Amish commitment of discipleship even to death remains strong. Theirs is a spirit of humility and awe before God the Creator and a willingness to give up "worldly" distractions so as to follow the teachings of Jesus more closely. The Amish are at peace with their convictions but do not look down on outsiders whose understandings lead to a different way of life.

The Crown of Thorns pattern is a series of triangles and squares making construction simple. However, the visual impact of the quilt is much more complex. Ornate quilting is reserved for non-pieced blocks and borders.

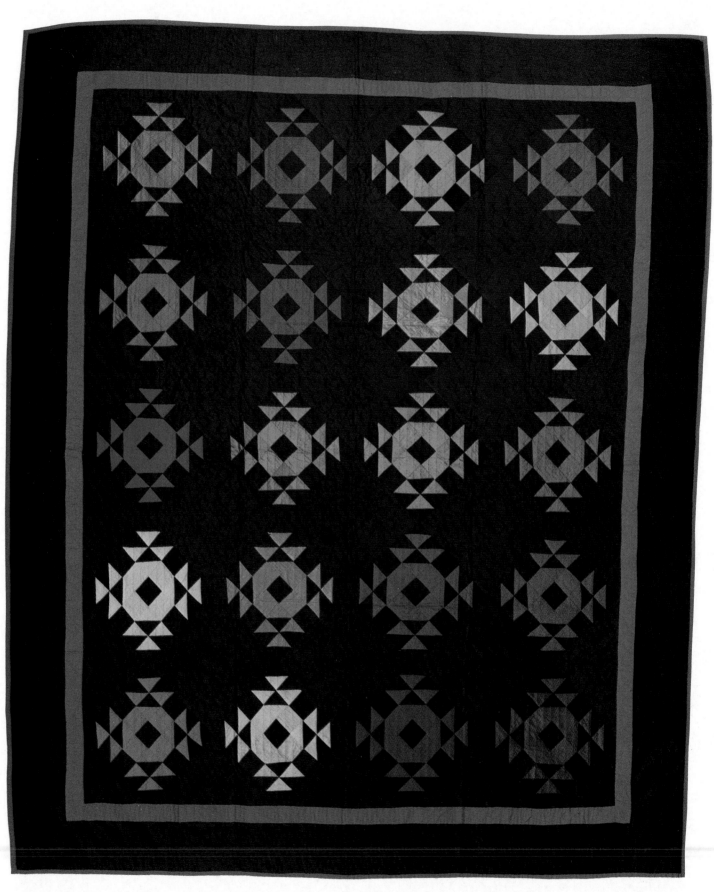

Crown of Thorns, c. 1930. Cotton sateen, 80 x 94. Holmes Co., Ohio. Collection of Catherine H. Anthony.

Crown of Thorns
Approximate size 90 x 104

Measurements given <u>without</u> seam allowance

A — template given

B — template given

C — cut 12 squares 10½ inches by 10½ inches

D — cut 14 triangles

10½ inches / 10½ inches

Make 20 pieced blocks

E — cut 4 triangles

7½ inches / 7½ inches

F — width of inner border 3 inches

G — width of outer border 12 inches

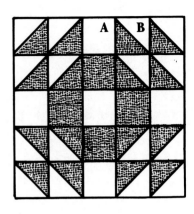

Assembly instructions:

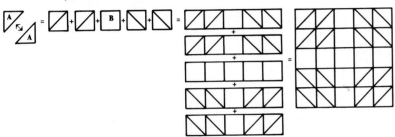

See Diagram 2, pg. 21 (Total Quilt Assembly).
See Border Application Diagram, pg. 23.

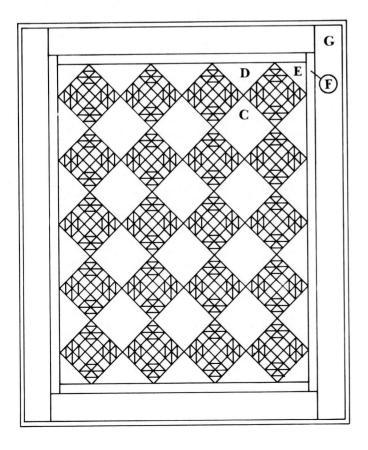

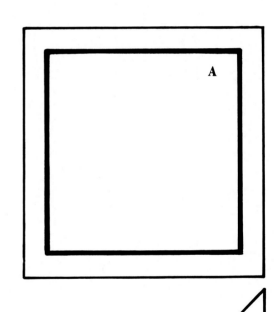

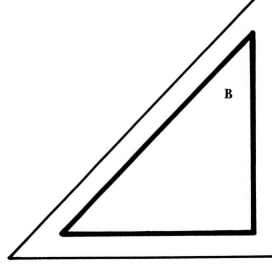

How To Make an Amish Quilt

Crown of Thorns
Approximate size 46 x 58

Measurements given <u>without</u> seam allowance

A — template given
B — template given
C — cut 2 squares 9 inches by 9 inches
D — cut 6 triangles

9 inches / 9 inches

E — cut 4 triangles

6⅜ inches / 6⅜ inches

F — width of inner border 2 inches
G — width of outer border 8 inches

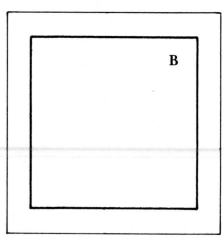

Assembly instructions:

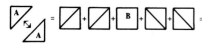

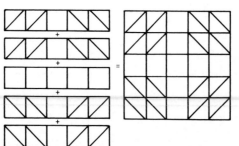

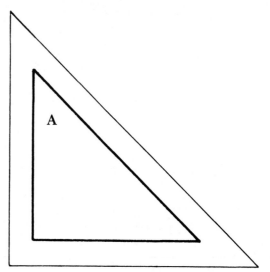

See Diagram 4, pg. 22 (Total Quilt Assembly).
See Border Application Diagram, pg. 23.

Bear Paw

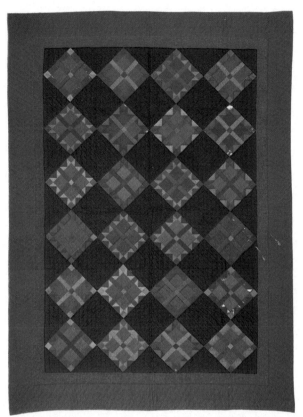

Cross and Crown, c. 1925. Cotton, 87 x 64. Elkhart Co., Indiana. Rebecca Haarer. This variation of the Bear Paw design places the outer triangles in an alternate direction.

The inspiration for the Bear Paw pattern is said to have come from frontier days when bear tracks were commonly found in the snow or mud of wooded farmland. An encounter with wildlife was a daily possibility and was captured in this quilt design. The pattern was borrowed by the Amish community and used largely by Midwestern Amish quilters. A slight variation of the pattern is also known as Cross and Crown. This name carries the religious significance of Jesus' death on the cross and the crown of thorns that he wore.

The pattern looks complex because of its jagged edges but the shapes make construction quite simple. Triangles forming the bear's toes are sewn together to form squares. The squares are connected to a larger square and rectangles form the connecting cross pieces.

This design's most realistic look is achieved when strongly contrasting colors are used making the paw stand out sharply against the background. Quilting generally outlines the paw shape and decorates alternate squares as well as the borders.

Bear Paw, dated 1939. Cotton, 85 x 71. Ohio. Judi Boisson Antique American Quilts, New York. The sawtooth inner border ties in nicely with the jagged Bear Paw design.

How To Make an Amish Quilt

Bear Paw, dated 1893. Cotton, 85 x 69. Loudenville, Ohio. Judi Boisson Antique American Quilts, New York. Quilting designs are not elaborate but are very extensive and excellently crafted. The red inner border and binding give life to this quilt.

Bear Paw, c. 1915. Cotton, 72 x 64. La-Grange Co., Indiana. Joseph M. B. Sarah.

How To Make an Amish Quilt

Bear Paw
Approximate size 90 x 104

Measurements given <u>without</u> seam allowance

A — template given
B — template given
C — template given
D — template given
E — cut 12 squares 10½ x 10½ inches
F — cut 14 triangles

G — cut 4 triangles

H — width of inner border 3 inches
I — width of outer border 12 inches

Make 20 pieced blocks

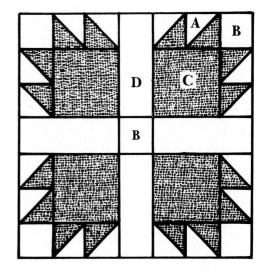

Assembly instructions:

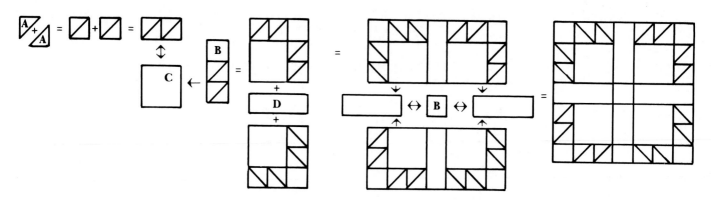

See Diagram 2, pg. 21 (Total Quilt Assembly).
See Border Application Diagram, pg. 23.

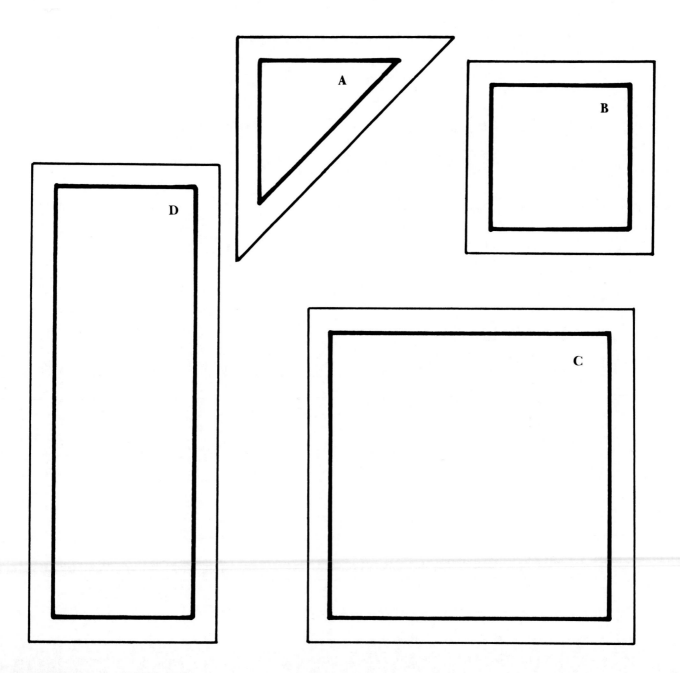

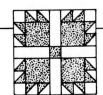

Bear Paw
Approximate size 46 x 58

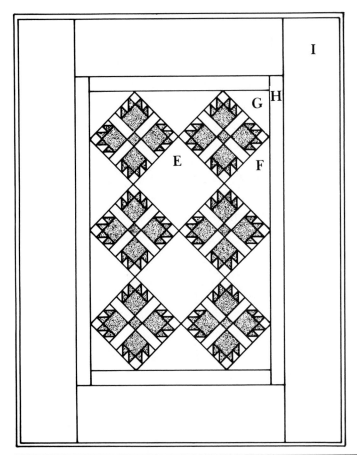

Measurements given <u>without</u> seam allowance

A — template given
B — template given
C — template given
D — template given
E — cut 2 squares 9 inches by 9 inches
F — cut 6 triangles

9 inches / 9 inches

G — cut 4 triangles

6⅜ inches / 6⅜ inches

H — width of inner border 2 inches
I — width of outer border 8 inches
Make 6 pieced blocks

Assembly instructions:

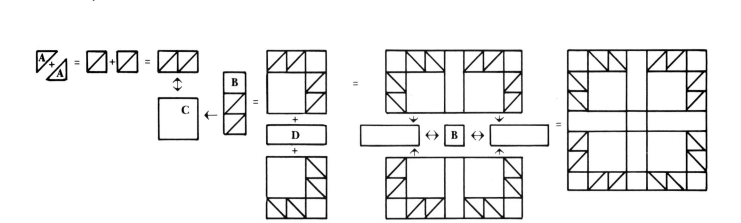

See Diagram 4, pg. 22 (Total Quilt Assembly).
See Border Application Diagram, pg. 23.

How To Make an Amish Quilt

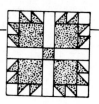

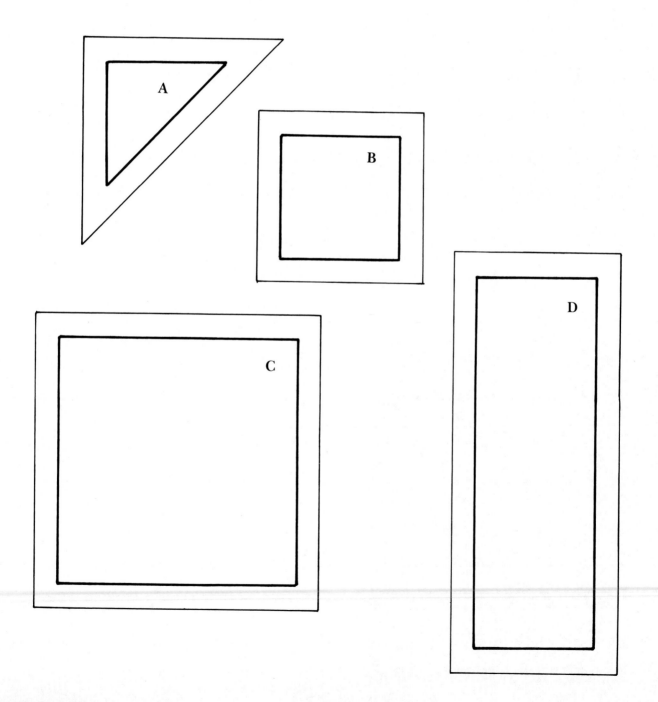

Pinwheel

Pinwheel Variation, dated February 12, 1925. Cotton, 76 x 66. LaGrange Co., Indiana. Rebecca Haarer. This variation is also called Twin Sisters.

Crazy Ann, dated March 1915. Cotton, 86 x 78. Topeka, LaGrange Co., Indiana. Rebecca Haarer. This Pinwheel variation has initials embroidered in the bottom right corner.

The windmill turns effortlessly in the breeze creating power to pump water to Amish houses and barns. The Amish have drawn fine but distinct lines on energy use.

They do not see electricity itself as wrong, but they do believe that purchasing it from local power companies links them physically to the larger world. Furthermore, such easy availability of electricity would present them with temptations that could undermine their family and community life—radio and television, for example, are seen as threatening.

By choosing to live without electricity, the Amish have become inventive in finding alternatives. They use gas, diesel, and pneumatic power to operate their refrigerators, kitchen appliances, and power tools. They live without electric lights, perhaps the greatest inconvenience modern Americans would feel in an Amish home. Instead, the Amish use gas lamps which provide bright and adequate light, but must be pumped, lit, and carried from room to room in the house. That choice in itself keeps a family physically together, evening after evening.

The Pinwheel quilt looks like the spinning blades of a windmill and is a gentle reminder of this less hurried and separate way of life. Although the pattern is used by many quiltmakers it seems to have a special link to the Amish. Triangles and rectangles form the pattern of blades and correct usage of color gives the illusion of movement. Pieced blocks are often alternated with solid blocks which encourage an energetic quilting caper. Borders are also clean open spaces waiting for the skilled artistry of the quilter.

How To Make an Amish Quilt

Pinwheel, dated 1929. Wool, 76½ x 67½. Elkhart Co., Indiana. Donna and Jonathan Speigel. Tulip designs are quilted on the plain patches between the pieced blocks.

How To Make an Amish Quilt

Pinwheel

Approximate size 90 x 104

Variation 1

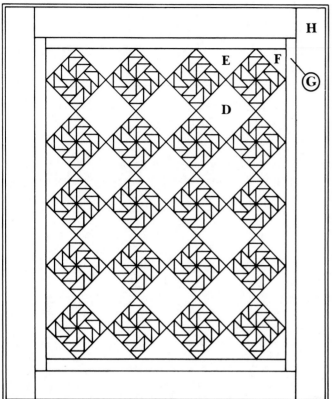

Measurements given <u>without</u> seam allowance

A — template given
B — template given
C — template given
D — cut 12 squares 10½ inches by 10½ inches
E — cut 14 triangles

F — cut 4 triangles

G — width of inner border 3 inches
H — width of outer border 12 inches

Make 20 pieced blocks

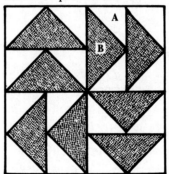

Assembly instructions:

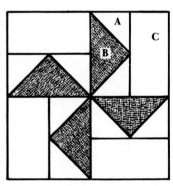

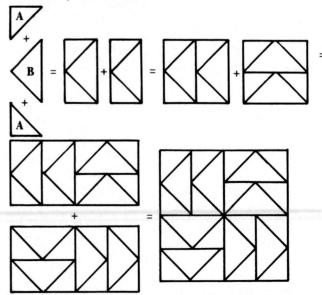

Variation 2

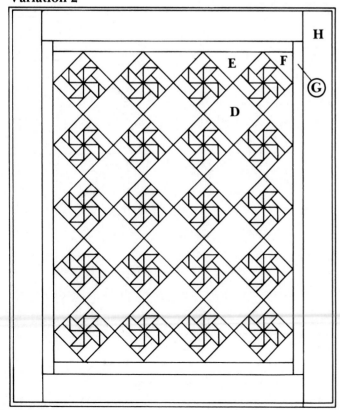

See Diagram 2, pg. 21 (Total Quilt Assembly).
See Border Application Diagram, pg. 23.

How To Make an Amish Quilt

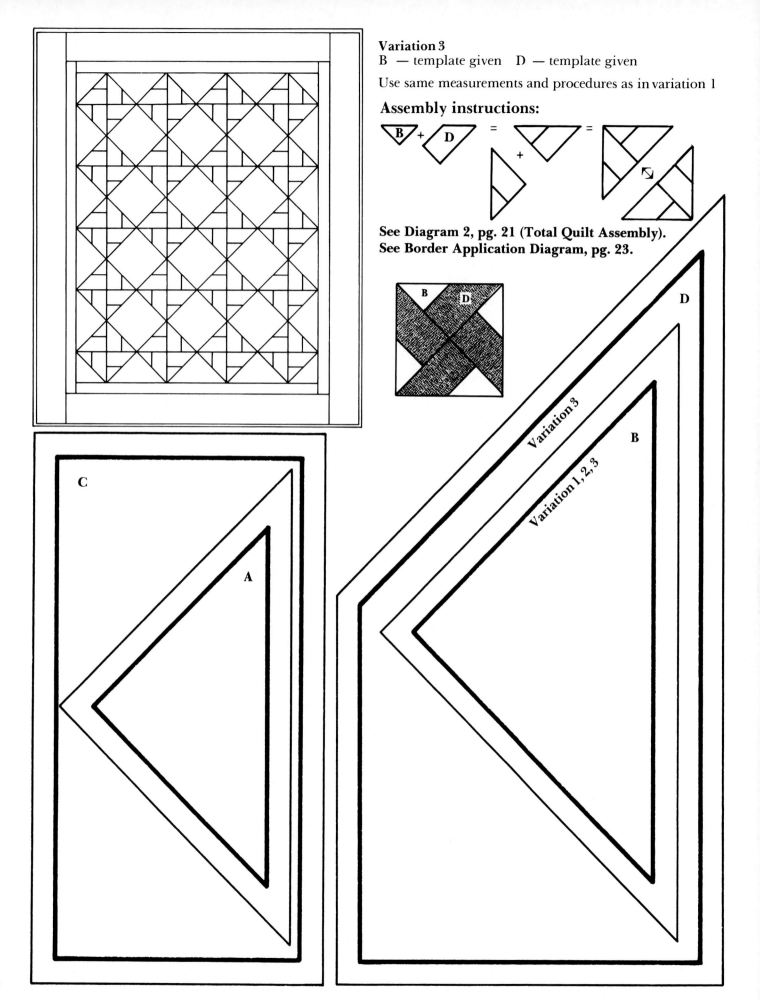

Variation 3

B — template given   D — template given

Use same measurements and procedures as in variation 1

Assembly instructions:

See Diagram 2, pg. 21 (Total Quilt Assembly).
See Border Application Diagram, pg. 23.

C

A

Variation 3

Variation 1, 2, 3

D

B

Pinwheel
Approximate size 46 x 58

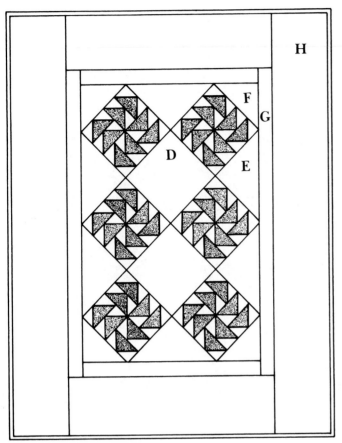

Variation 1

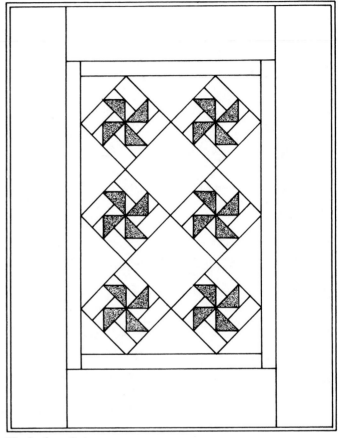

Variation 2

Measurements given <u>without</u> seam allowance

A — template given
B — template given
C — template given (used in variation 2)
D — cut 2 squares 9 inches x 9 inches
E — cut 6 triangles

9 inches (vertical) / 9 inches (horizontal)

F — cut 4 triangles

6⅜ inches (vertical) / 6⅜ inches (horizontal)

G — width of inner border 2 inches
H — width of outer border 8 inches
Make 6 pieced blocks

Assembly instructions:

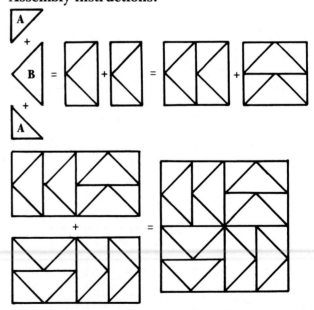

See Diagram 4, pg. 22 (Total Quilt Assembly).
See Border Application Diagram, pg. 23.

How To Make an Amish Quilt

Variation 3 Approximate size 46x58

B — template given
J — template given
Use same measurements and procedures as in
variation 1

Assembly instructions:

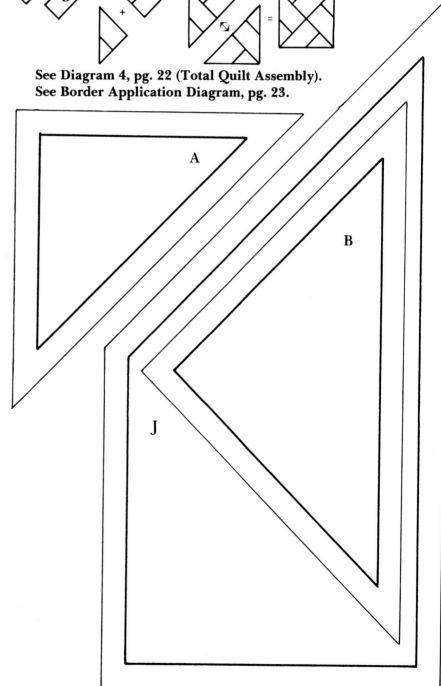

See Diagram 4, pg. 22 (Total Quilt Assembly).
See Border Application Diagram, pg. 23.

Garden Maze

Rolling Stone in Garden Maze, c. 1910-20. Cotton, 67 x 78. Collected Elkhart Co., Indiana. Harry Brorby.

Garden Maze describes a pattern of square fabric blocks, each surrounded by elaborate sashing. The two narrow borders that outline each square connect neighboring squares and intersect between their corners. Although the inside square could be left empty, it is commonly filled with a pieced design. The pieced design and the surrounding maze are usually contained within a quilted border.

The Garden Maze quilt is as neat and orderly as an Amish garden. Few gardeners surpass the meticulous care given by Amish growers. Rows are straight and neat. Flowers often surround the garden edge giving it a burst of bright color. Weeds are nipped in the bud and plants are carefully tended. For many women, spring fever and garden fever come hand in hand and they eagerly await the chance to work in the soil.

Although gardening is thoroughly enjoyed by many Amish families, it is not just a hobby. Preservation of food occupies a large part of the women's energies throughout the summer and by the onset of winter their larders are full of canned, pickled, and preserved vegetables, relishes, jams, fruits, and meats.

Quilting takes a back seat to these seasonal requirements. But in the fall and winter when days are spent indoors, quilting resumes at full force. It is a happy balance when the necessary work of life is so wholeheartedly enjoyed and incorporated into their more relaxed tasks. The Amish seem to have mastered this art in many areas.

Men help most in preparation of the soil for the family garden. Here two sons help ready the garden for planting while the team rests in the shade, waiting for another stint in the fields.

How To Make an Amish Quilt

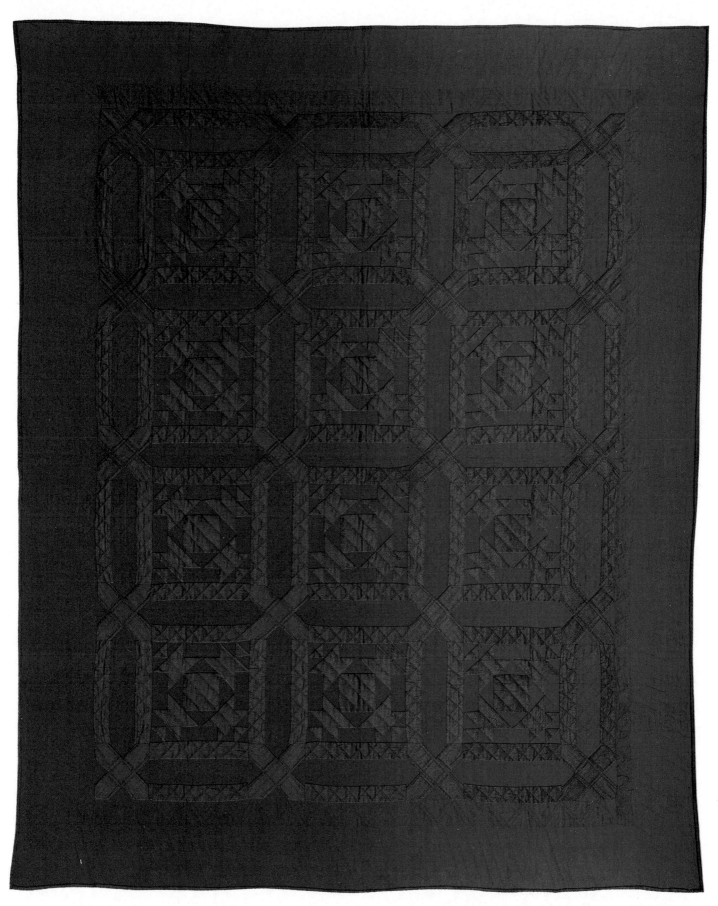

Cups and Saucers in Garden Maze, c. 1919. Cotton, wool, 83 x 68. LaGrange Co., Indiana. Rebecca Haarer. The Garden Maze is the sash work surrounding the smaller pieced designs.

Garden Maze
Approximate size 86 x 103

Measurements given <u>without</u> seam allowance
A — template given
B — template given
C — template given
D — template given
E — template given
F — cut 12 squares 10 inches by 10 inches
G — width of inner border 3 inches
H — width of outer border 12 inches

Assembly instructions:

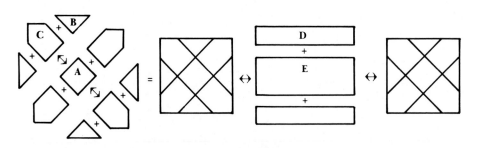

See Diagram 1, pg. 21 (Total Quilt Assembly)
See Border Application Diagram, pg. 23.

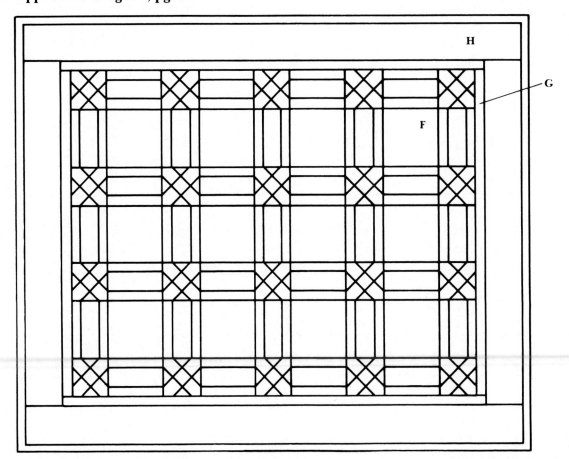

How To Make an Amish Quilt

Garden Maze
Approximate size 48 x 60

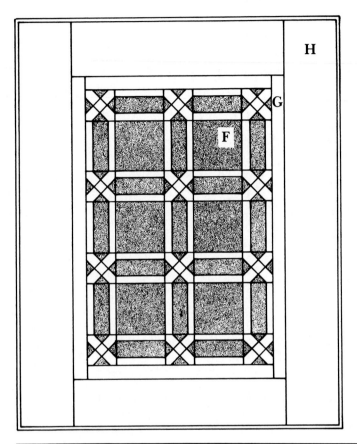

Measurements given <u>without</u> seam allowance

A — template given
B — template given
C — template given
D — template given
E — template given
F — cut 6 squares 7½ inches x 7½ inches
G — width of inner border 2 inches
H — width of outer border 8 inches

Assembly instructions:

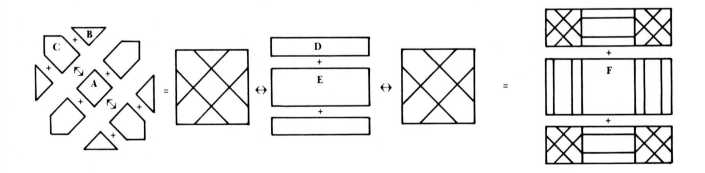

See Diagram 3, pg. 22 (Total Quilt Assembly).
See Border Application Diagram, pg. 23.

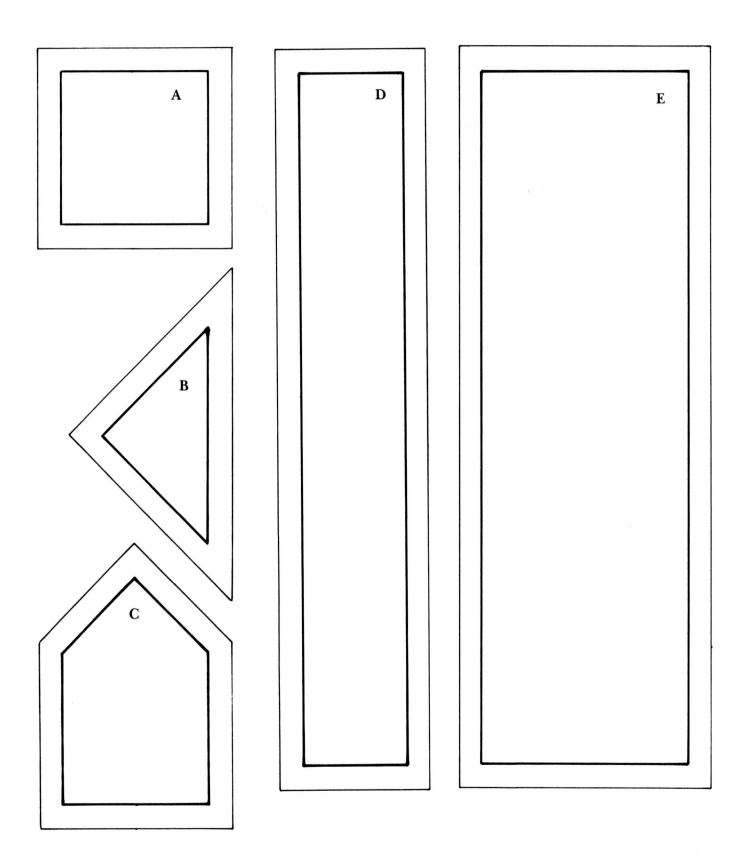

A

B

C

D

E

A Quilting

For a people who choose to do without radio, TV, movies, and many types of entertainment enjoyed by the larger society, visiting is vital. Visiting happens regularly and spontaneously. Unannounced guests are always welcome. Even if a visit happens to be near mealtime, the company is heartily invited to stay and eat. Families often spend Sunday afternoons or evenings with relatives or friends. It is the slower pace of the Amish lifestyle that allows time for the simple pleasures of human interaction. Gathered friends may play games together or, more likely, talk about events in each other's lives.

Quiltings Mix Work and Visiting

A quilting is an all-day occasion to do some fun "work"—and visit. It is generally hosted by a woman who has one or more quilts to quilt. She may choose to make it a "sisters day" whereupon she invites all her sisters, or she may issue a broader invitation to specific friends and neighbors. Quiltings take place throughout the year but they are more frequent during less busy seasons on the farm.

Usually quilting begins early in the morning after mothers have given their school-age children a proper breakfast and seen them off for the day. Pre-school children attend quiltings, and since there are usually a group of them, have as much fun playing as their mothers have quilting. Older children may be asked to keep a supply of threaded needles on hand and they help to watch their younger siblings. The quilt, stretched tightly in a quilting frame, provides a wonderful imaginary house for these youngsters.

"Putting In" the Quilt

The first job to be done (if the hostess has not already completed it) is "putting in" the quilt. That involves stretching the back, lining, and top of the quilt tautly in the frame. The most common type of frame allows quilters to work on all four sides of the quilt at the same time. It is a simple structure with four strips of wood held together by C-clamps. The top and bottom ends of the quilt back are pinned or basted to a strip of heavy fabric which has been tacked along the edge of two of the frame's wooden strips. The back is then tightly stretched between these two strips and the remaining two wooden strips are laid along the sides of the quilt back. The pieces of wood are clamped at the corners, thus making the quilt back a tight, flat surface. The frame, now stretched to its proper size, is then laid across the backs of four chairs making it an appropriate height for quilting. Next, the lining is laid on the quilt back and pinned securely on all sides. And finally the top, with its tracings for quilting designs, is stretched over the back and lining and pinned tightly in place. The bedcover is ready to be quilted.

A Quilting Pecking Order

A typical quilting will involve anywhere from six to twelve women. Seating positions around the quilting frame are often good-naturedly negotiated since no one wants to sit next to and be outshone by the best or fastest quilter! And less experienced quilters choose to sit where there are straight lines to quilt since they are more easily managed than curved lines.

How To Make an Amish Quilt

This detail shows five typical quilting designs: 1) pumpkin seed, 2) cross hatch, 3) cable, 4) fan, and 5) feather.

Quilting templates are often made from scrap pieces of cardboard. After the design is cut away, the pattern is traced on the quilt top and then covered with tiny stitches.

The women, sitting around all four sides of the frame, begin quilting at the outer edge and work toward the center as far as they are able to reach. When all the women along the top and bottom of the frame have quilted to their maximum stretch, the quilt is ready to "roll." The clamps at the four corners of the frame are released and the finished sections of the quilt are gently rolled onto the wood until the unquilted surface is brought to the edge. "Rolling" can take place only from the two ends of the frame. Therefore, when the quilters along the side reach their maximum they must either find and squeeze into a new position at the ends, begin another quilt in another frame, or find something else to do. Those who choose the latter frequently help the hostess prepare lunch.

Eating Belongs with a Quilting

The noon meal is compensation for the time and effort supplied by the invited quilters. It is a highlight of the day. The hostess prepares a full-course meal and serves it with pride. Kitchen helpers may be women who were invited to the quilting but would rather not quilt. For them, being in the kitchen is as enjoyable as being around the frame. However, if a woman is assigned to kitchen duty when she would rather quilt, it can be humbling. This sometimes happens to teenaged girls whose stitches are not yet tiny or neat enough to meet the hostess' quilting standards. It is an honor for young girls to be invited to quilt at a quilting. Quilting resumes again after lunch. Women are free to come and go as they are able. Some stay the whole day. Others come for only a few hours.

A Strengthening Time

A quilting is more than a work day. It is an occasion to share household tips, garden hints, home remedies, child-rearing information, and the latest news about marriages, births, and deaths. Such a gathering of women with common backgrounds, interests, and goals provides a chance for them to talk at length about their daily lives. A quilting reminds these women of the support they have and gives them a break from daily routine. For hard-working farm women, such an event can be a refreshing one-day vacation.

Quilting for Others

Quiltings are not only held in private homes. The Amish, though separate from the larger world, are not unaware of global needs. Amish women readily participate in quiltings held by the Mennonite Central Committee, a world-wide relief organization that sends food, clothing, and personnel all over the world. Amish women also lend their skills to community projects. Many volunteer fire companies hold quiltings several times a year to produce quilts to sell at their benefit auctions. Since the Amish rely on the services of their local fire companies, they support them actively as volunteer firefighters and contribute time and energy to their quiltings and benefit suppers.

When a quilting day is ended and the quilt completed, it stands as a tangible symbol of group effort. It portrays not only the skill of these women, but also the strong supportive love that envelops this community and keeps it vibrant and alive despite the pressures of the modern world.

Railroad Crossing

The Railroad Crossing pattern, when used by Amish quilters, is found mainly among Midwestern Amish. This pattern varies extensively. The "crossings" become the main focus when a series of narrow horizontal strips resembling railroad ties are assembled. In other variations the main emphasis is on the space between the "crossings" which is broken into a collage of brightly colored triangles. The entire pieced top is framed with one or more borders.

Although most travel by the Amish is limited to horse-drawn carriages, they are permitted to use public transportation. Many Amish take advantage of local bus routes and for extended travel will use trains.

It is also common for them to hire a van and driver for a fee who then serve much like a taxi with the family or families having direct control of its route. This allows them to make stops for visiting or shopping enroute to their destination. In areas with high concentrations of Amish there are usually several persons who offer van service. For short trips to town or to a doctor where use of the carriage is not practical it is not unusual for the Amish to hire their non-Amish neighbors to drive them.

Railroad Crossing, dated 1928. Cotton, 86 x 61. Holmes Co., Ohio. The Darwin D. Bearley Collection. This variation uses a pinwheel patch in the center of each block surrounded by stacked triangles. A zig-zag inner border adds to the drama of this quilt.

Railroad Crossing, c. 1920. Cotton, 75 x 79. Holmes Co., Ohio. Judi Boisson Antique American Quilts, New York. Unusually light colors are used throughout this quilt. Although the patches vary, their color schemes are obviously planned in a similar fashion.

How To Make an Amish Quilt

Railroad Crossing Variation, dated March 5, 1943. Cotton, 66 x 84. Denton, Ohio. Judi Boisson Antique American Quilts, New York.

Railroad Crossing Variation, c. 1925-30. Cotton, 92 x 76. Elkhart Co., Indiana. Joseph M. B. Sarah. *The consistent arrangement of strips in this pattern show careful planning. A touch of yellow in the pattern is highlighted by the narrow yellow border framing the piecework.*

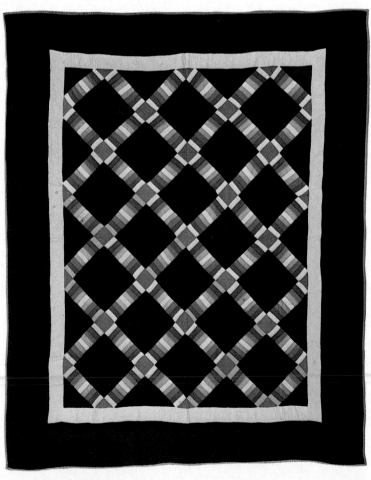

How To Make an Amish Quilt

Railroad Crossing
Approximate size 92 x 112

Measurements given <u>without</u> seam allowance

A — template given
B — template given
C — cut 18 squares 10 inches by 10 inches
D — cut 10 triangles

10 inches
10 inches

E — template given
F — template given
G — width of inner border 3 inches
H — width of outer border 12 inches

Assembly instructions:

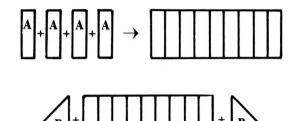

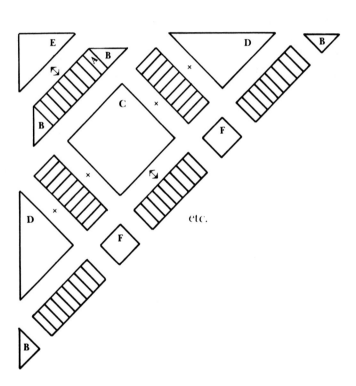

See Border Application Diagram, pg. 23.

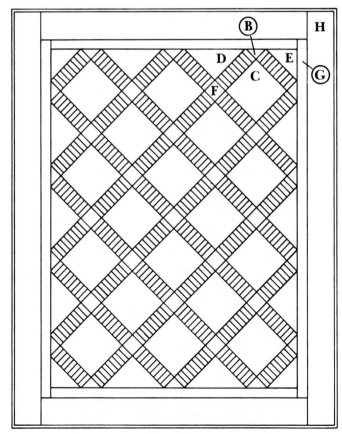

Railroad Crossing
Approximate size 48 × 62

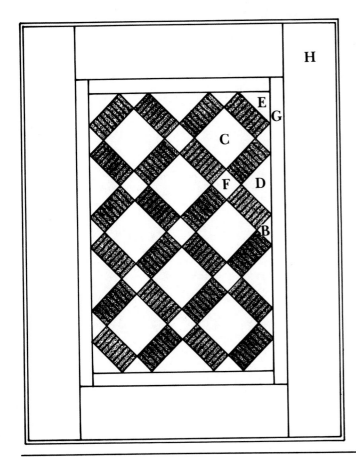

Measurements given <u>without</u> seam allowance

A—template given
B—template given
C—cut 8 squares 6¾ inches by 6¾ inches
D—template given
E—template given
F—template given
G—width of inner border 2 inches
H—width of outer border 8 inches

Assembly instructions:

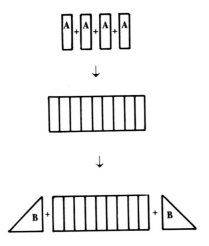

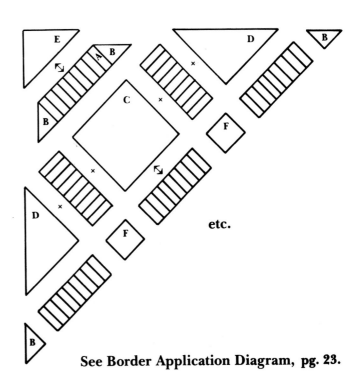

etc.

See Border Application Diagram, pg. 23.

How To Make an Amish Quilt

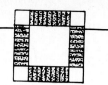

A

B

D

E

F

Double Wedding Ring

Double Wedding Ring, 1953. Cotton, 82 x 88. Arthur, Illinois. Rebecca Haarer. The white background and scalloped edge mark this as a later quilt. Although the date marks this quilt as later than most collected antique Amish quilts, it is included here as an example of a less conservative approach to color.

The Double Wedding Ring is a design of great complexity and openness requiring much of its maker. Its light, airy feeling is achieved by interlocking pieced rings that surround circular fields that invite intricate quilting. The pattern must have been borrowed by Amish quiltmakers seeking a real challenge in piecing. The Double Wedding Ring pattern is difficult to execute because all sides of the patch are curved. This requires precision in both cutting and piecing so that the finished top will lay flat without gathers or puckers.

Quilting generally outlines the angled pieces within the rings plus creates an additional design inside each ring. Amish Double Wedding Ring quilts generally have borders that also contain generous quilting.

It is easy to understand the popularity of this design in general society. It is an appropriate choice for a wedding gift. However, in Amish circles, jewelry of all kinds, including wedding bands, is not permitted. So the Amish quiltmakers' fascination with this pattern must have been because of its complexity.

Although the Amish do not use wedding rings, they view marriage as a serious commitment, made for life. Divorce is almost unheard of among Amish groups. Marriages last because of the support system provided by a couple's families and church. They do not marry and rear children in isolation. They are nurtured and tended by a closeknit group of concerned friends who share a common faith-life.

Farmsteads often house three generations and although privacy is maintained by the third generation having separate quarters, grandparents, parents, and children have a great deal of interaction. One's closest neighbors are often family or other church members. Together they share in life's joys and sorrows.

Interlocking circular images are found in many places around the farm. Resembling the Double Wedding Ring pattern, the wheels of this implement serve important functions on Amish farmsteads.

How To Make an Amish Quilt

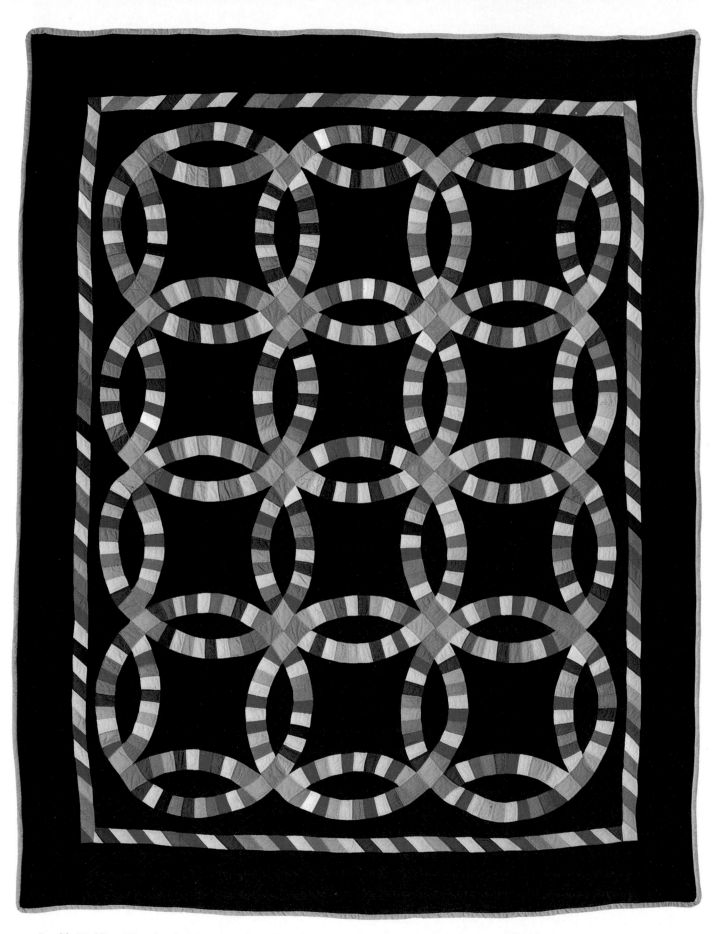

Double Wedding Ring, dated 1952. Cotton, 73 x 93. Holmes Co., Ohio. Judi Boisson Antique American Quilts, New York. Bright colors stand out vividly against a black background. Pieced diamonds form a containing inner border. Spider web quilting designs fill the centers of the rings. Although a later quilt, it is done in colors typical of earlier Amish quilts in this pattern.

How To Make an Amish Quilt

Double Wedding Ring
Approximate size 90 x 103

A — template given
B — template given
C — template given
D — template given
E — template given
F — template given

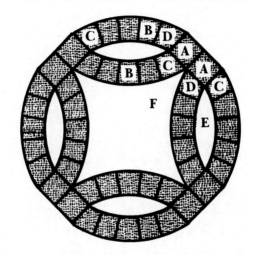

Assembly instructions:

 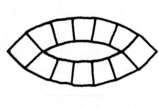

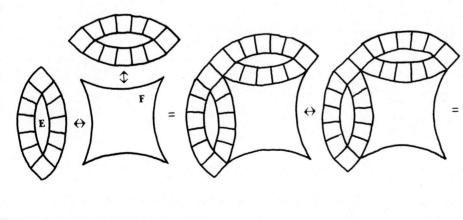

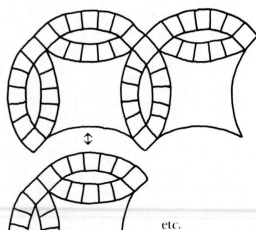

etc.

How To Make an Amish Quilt

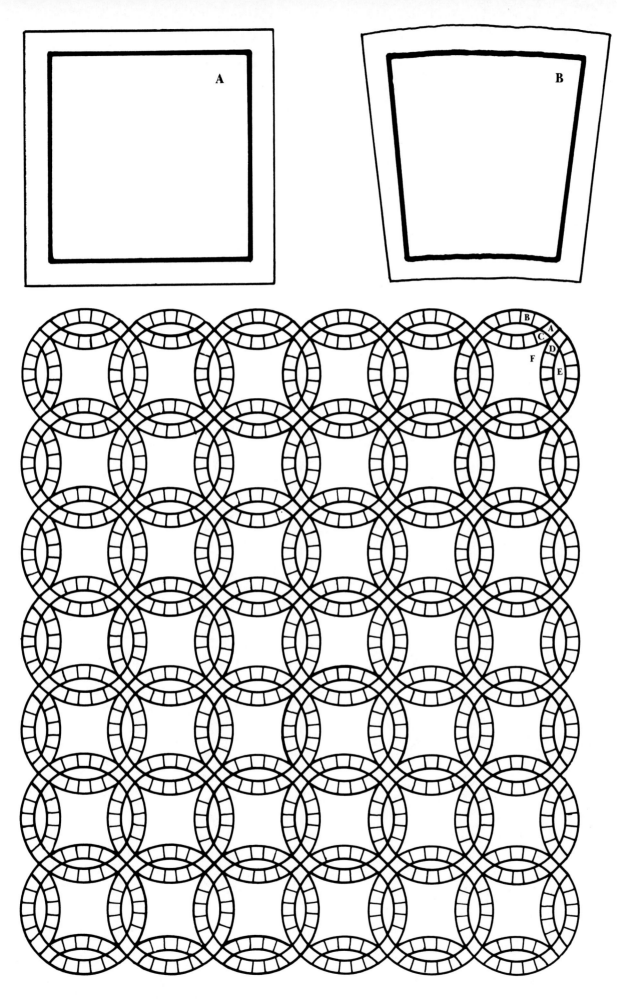

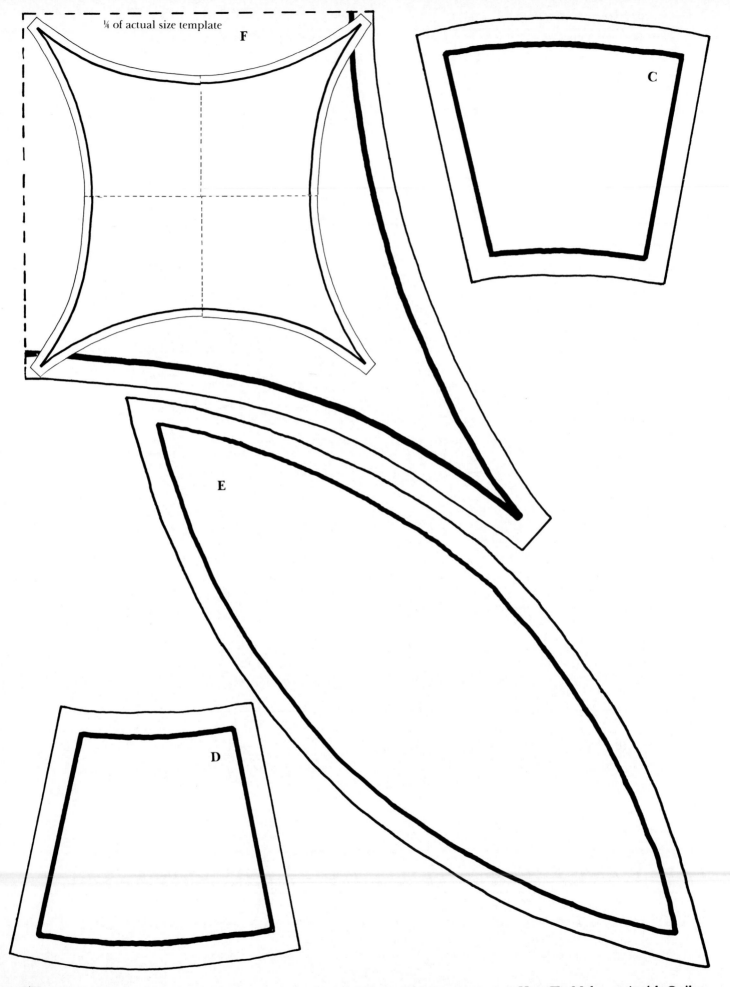

¼ of actual size template

F

C

E

D

How To Make an Amish Quilt

Double Wedding Ring
Approximate size 40 x 58

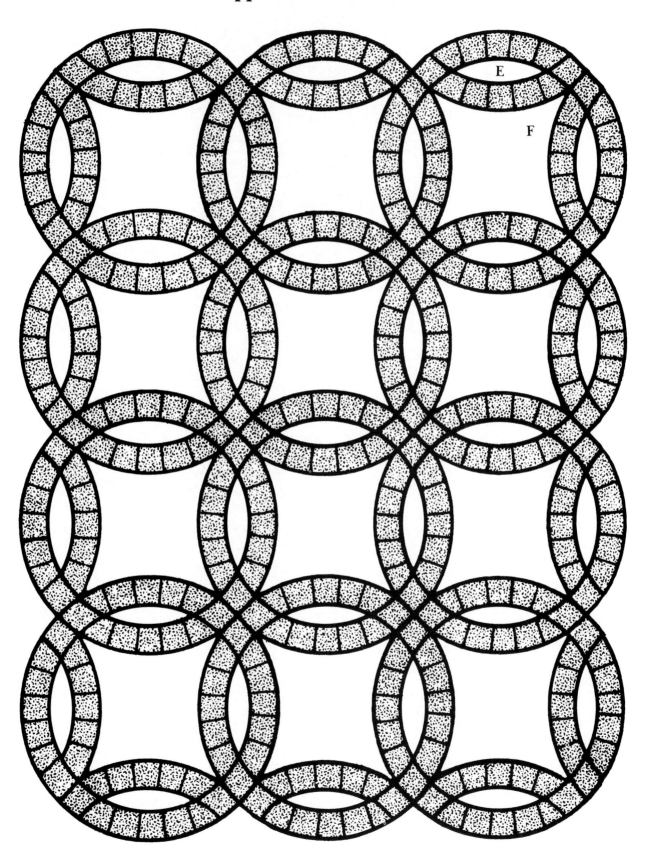

A — template given
B — template given
C — template given
D — template given
E — template given
F — template given

Assembly instructions:

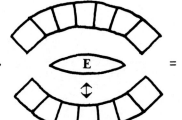

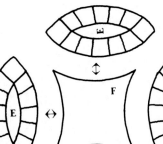

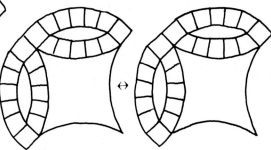

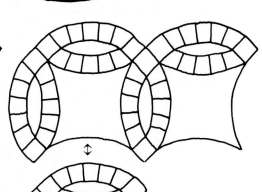

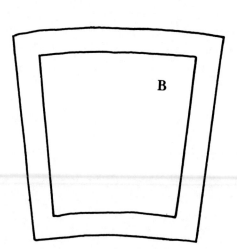

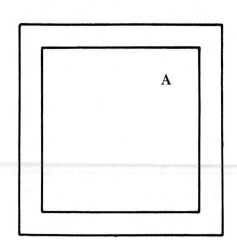

A

B

How To Make an Amish Quilt

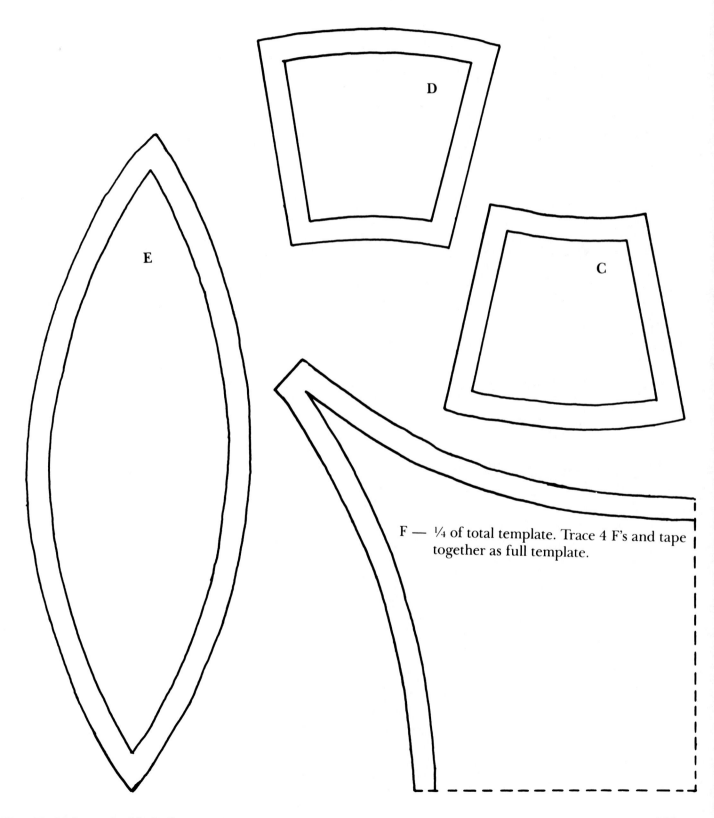

D

E

C

F — ¼ of total template. Trace 4 F's and tape together as full template.

Diagonal Triangles

Triangles have always seemed to delight quilters. The angles and sharp points give a quilt vibrance and energy. Triangles appear in numerous complex patterns but are perfectly capable of standing alone. In the Diagonal Triangles pattern, light and dark triangles are pitted against each other forming jagged diagonal lines that shoot across the quilt top.

This quilt sparkles without fancy quilting. Its borders usually are filled with the typical Amish patterns of flowing quilting designs. The pieced body of the quilt generally has its triangles outlined in quilting stitches or simple straight lines are quilted across its top.

Diagonal Triangles, 1929. Cotton, 76 x 70. Holmes Co., Ohio. Judi Boisson Antique American Quilts, New York. Several streaks of red give real zest to this dramatic quilt.

Diagonal Triangles, 1920-30. Cotton, 70 x 71. Holmes Co., Ohio. Judi Boisson Antique American Quilts, New York. An inner border of pieced diamonds outlines the sharp diagonal lines.

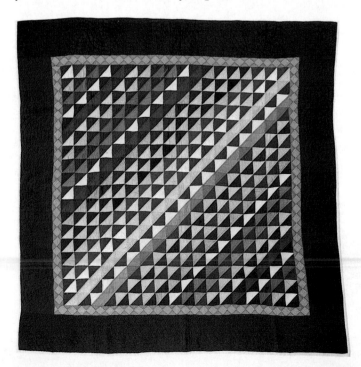

How To Make an Amish Quilt

Diagonal Triangles
Approximate size 90 x 96

Measurements given <u>without</u> seam allowance
A — template given
B — width of inner border 3 inches
C — width of outer border 12 inches

Assembly instructions:

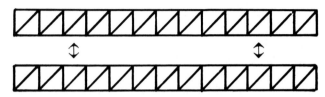

See Border Application Diagram, **pg. 23.**

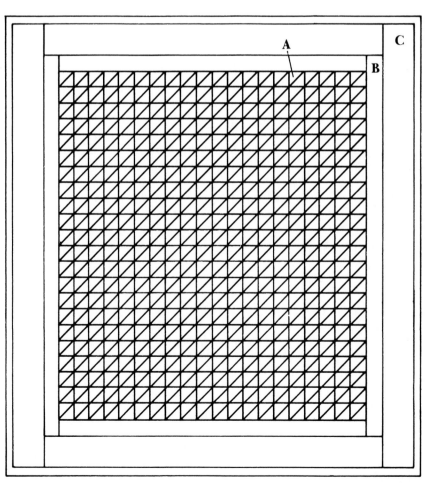

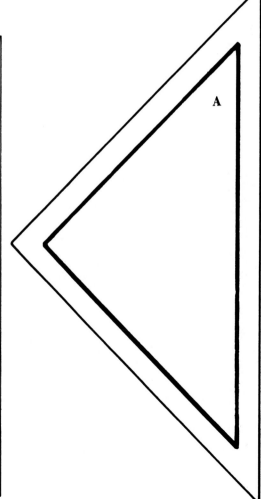

Drunkard's Path

Perhaps because the name has a negative connotation, perhaps because there are so many ways to organize it, this quilt has been called by an assortment of titles. Drunkard's Path is also known as Solomon's Puzzle, Old Maid Puzzle, Rocky Road to Kansas, Love Ring, None-Such, World Without End, and more.

No matter its name or arrangement it is a fascinating pattern. The blocks are a combination of positive and negative space. The section cut out of one patch creates a space to be filled by the adjoining patch. The result is a staggering path of patches across the quilt.

Piecing requires skill here because each patch has a curved edge. Care must be taken so that curves are smooth and flat. Assembly of the pieced blocks also demands clear thinking so that a consistent overall pattern is formed.

Quilting stitches generally follow the lines of the pieced design giving it an additional dimension. Empty space between patches and on borders provides additional space for quilting designs.

Drunkard's Path, c. 1935-40. Cotton, 79 x 86. Collected LaGrange Co., probably made there. Rebecca Haarer. This is also a friendship quilt. Various patches were likely constructed by the persons whose names are embroidered on them. The patches were then collected and assembled by or for a common friend.

Drunkard's Path Variation, c. 1910. Cotton, 80 x 75. Ohio. Judi Boisson Antique American Quilts, New York. This assemblage of Drunkard's Path patches is also known as "World Without End," or "Ocean Waves."

How To Make an Amish Quilt

Drunkard's Path, 1920-30. Cotton, 84 x 80. Withee, Wisconsin. Judi Boisson Antique American Quilts, New York. The addition of a sawtooth inner border brings angularity to an otherwise curved design.

Drunkard's Path

Approximate size 102 x 128

Measurements given <u>without</u> seam allowance

A — template given
B — template given
C — width of inner border 3 inches
D — width of outer border 9 inches

Make 192 pieced blocks. Alternate placement of blocks
to match diagram.

How To Make an Amish Quilt

Assembly instructions:

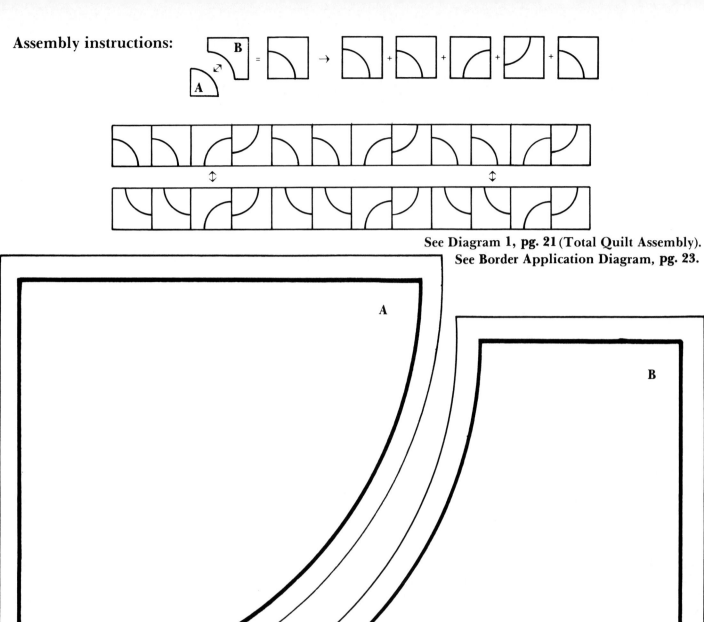

See Diagram 1, **pg. 21** (Total Quilt Assembly).
See Border Application Diagram, **pg. 23.**

Drunkard's Path
Approximate size 48 x 62

Measurements given <u>without</u> seam allowance

A— template given
B— template given
C— width of inner border 2 inches
D— width of outer border 8 inches
Make 96 pieced blocks. Alternate placement of
blocks to match diagram.

Assembly instructions:

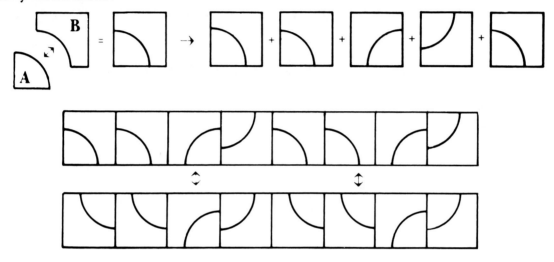

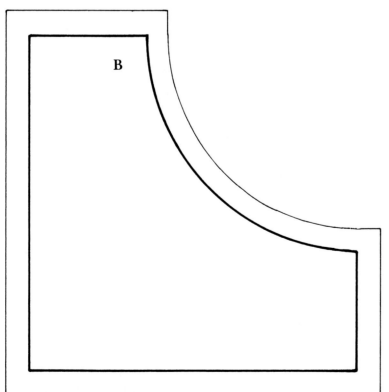

See Diagram 3, pg. 22 (Total Quilt Assembly).
See Border Application Diagram, pg. 23.

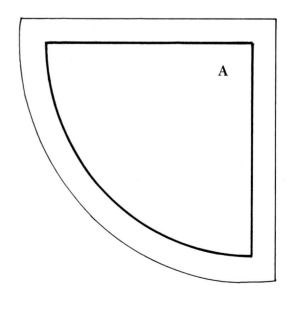

How To Make an Amish Quilt

Children are considered a gift from God by the Amish. They learn the joy, obedience and difficulty of the Amish way from the time they are born.

Contentment within Limitations

Being *in* the world but not *of* the world is a concept understood and practiced by the Amish in a radical way. This separateness is evidenced in their mode of dress, different language and independent school systems. They maintain these lines through a strong community and personal accountability to the brotherhood.

Most North Americans find their sense of personal worth in their job and its accomplishments. They thrive on a strong spirit of competition. But in the Amish world, values are different. Personal fulfillment is found within the group. Individualism is not erased but it is tempered by the goals and purposes of the community of faith. The good of the community is placed above one's personal gain. Being at peace with limitations is crucial to being Amish. Yet it seems that it is these very disciplines that inspire their creativity. Witness the ways the Amish have invented to maintain their lines of separateness without causing paralyzing hardships for themselves.

Living Without Electricity

Most Amish do not use electrical power from their local utility works. But that does not mean they are without energy. Many Amish are dairy farmers who must keep their milk cool while it waits to be picked up by a tank truck. So most use diesel driven refrigeration units, thus bypassing the need for electricity from high tension lines.

Increasingly more and more equipment is being attached to these diesel motors. In some communities it is common to rig up an air compressor to the motor. Air lines are run to the barn, shop, house and well. Adapters have been designed by Amish craftsmen to permit drills, lathes and many other kinds of hand and stationary equipment to be pneumatically powered. An air line to the bottom of the farm well supplies water to the house and barn. And in the house, mixers, blenders and washing machines may be energized by the same air compressor connected to the diesel motor that cools the bulk milk tank.

On farms without air compressors, water may be pumped by a windmill to a reservoir. This reservoir is often an up-ended tank train car placed at the top of the barnhill or some other point of high elevation. Simple gravity then supplies water to the barn and household.

Again, any generalization overlooks exceptions. Some Amish do use their local electrical company, others continue to reject the use of diesel motors for cooling milk.

How To Make an Amish Quilt

Strong Lines Create Energy Within

Many outsiders find these inventions to be grossly inconsistent. But to understand these people one must not forget the Amish community's intent—to draw clearly defined lines that provide solidarity for the group and separation from the world.

Belonging to a group with well-defined rules could seem stifling. And yet when perimeters are outlined, members find freedom to move around within them. When they agree with and understand the guidelines, they tap their own ingenuity to find resourceful ways to be content. The Amish farmer does not envy his non-Amish neighbor who plows with a tractor. He knows a tractor is not an option. He sets his mind to enjoy farming the Amish way. His responsibility is to be a good steward of God's earth. And his perception of how to accomplish that task has been formed within the context of a group who supports and shares his values.

On Amish farms, young and old, male and female help with field and garden work. It is common to see women in command of a team of horses and mules in the field.

Finding Beauty in the Simple

The Amish have developed a character of contentment. They enjoy the basics of life without thinking about the ruffles. For example, their food is usually prepared in standard, sturdy ways. They haven't nurtured a romance with fancy cuisine. Instead, robust food in plentiful quantity is the rule.

Nor is decorating a major concern of Amish women. This does not mean they have no aesthetic appreciation. Amish homes frequently contain beautifully handpainted chairs and chests. Most women own a set of decorated china and pieces of it are often displayed on a buffet or server when it is not in use. Handpainted mottos hang on bare walls. And in general, homes are meticulously clean and tidy.

Even in the clothing that Amish women make for themselves and their families, although it follows a prescribed pattern, there is evident a sense of pride in doing it well.

Children, who grow up without television and few mass-produced, store-bought toys, learn early to have fun instead with their imagination and many brothers and sisters. A farm—and animals—offer many possibilities for play.

The Amish world is not perfect. For instance, Amish families struggle with relationships and economic tensions like their non-Amish neighbors. But the Amish do not need to face their problems in isolation. They have each other for strength and understanding.

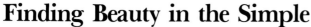

The Amish caution on modern technology has resulted in their own collection of inventions. Here is a hydraulic plow, complete with padded seat, which remains within the church regulations that stipulate steel wheels.

Quilting Templates

Following are several traditional quilting templates given in full size. Many of the templates extend over several pages. To use, make photocopies or tracings of template sections. Match corresponding letters along dotted lines and tape pages together to form the complete template.

One quarter of the Circular Feather is given. To make a complete circle, trace the section given, make a one-quarter turn, and trace again. Repeat until circle is complete.

Circular Feather — i.

To create finished template, match corresponding letters along dotted lines, and tape.

Completed pattern motif will look like this:

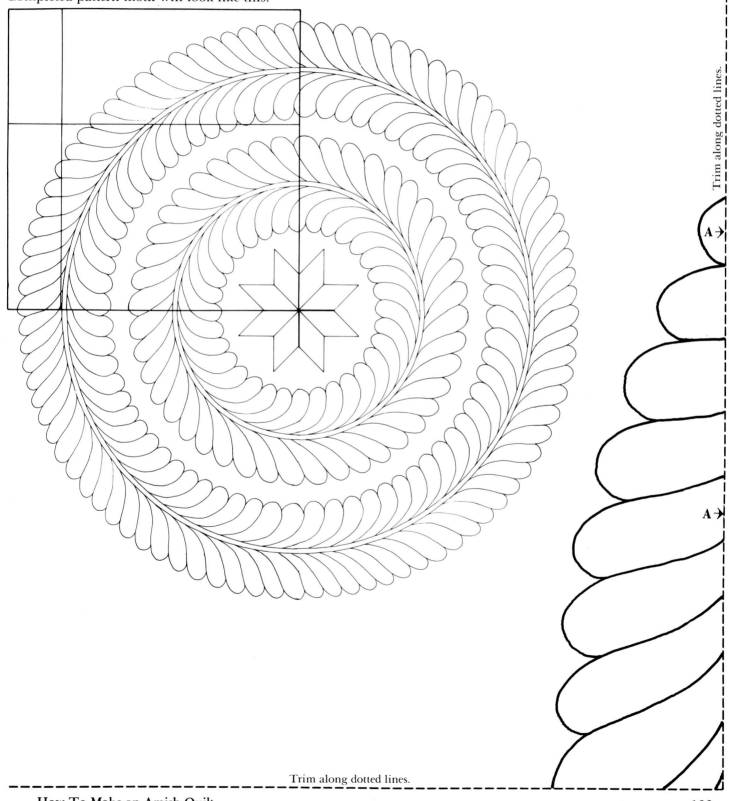

Circular Feather — ii.

Circular Feather — iii.

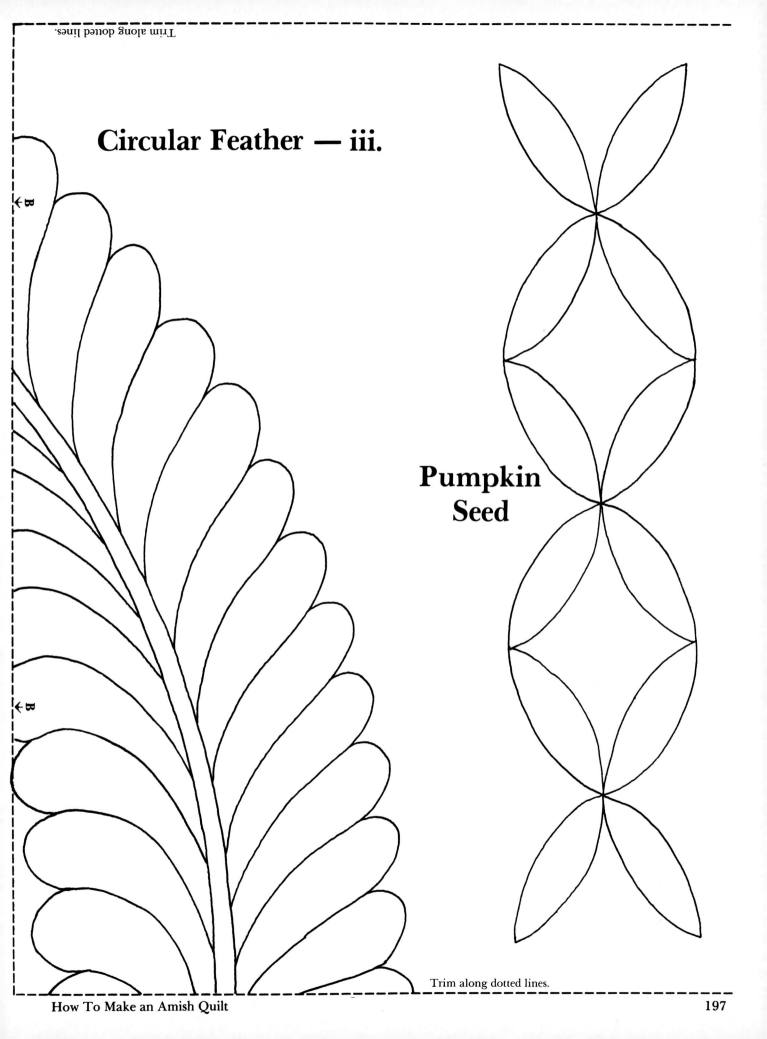

B

B

Pumpkin Seed

Trim along dotted lines.

Triangular Rose — i.

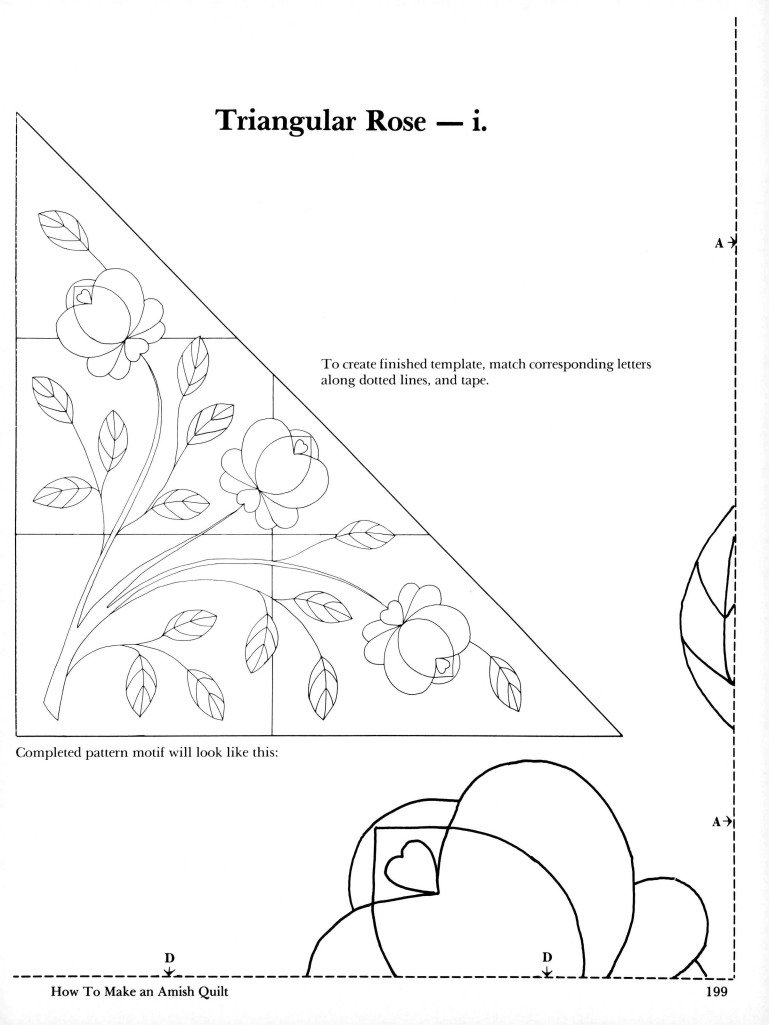

To create finished template, match corresponding letters along dotted lines, and tape.

Completed pattern motif will look like this:

Triangular Rose — ii.

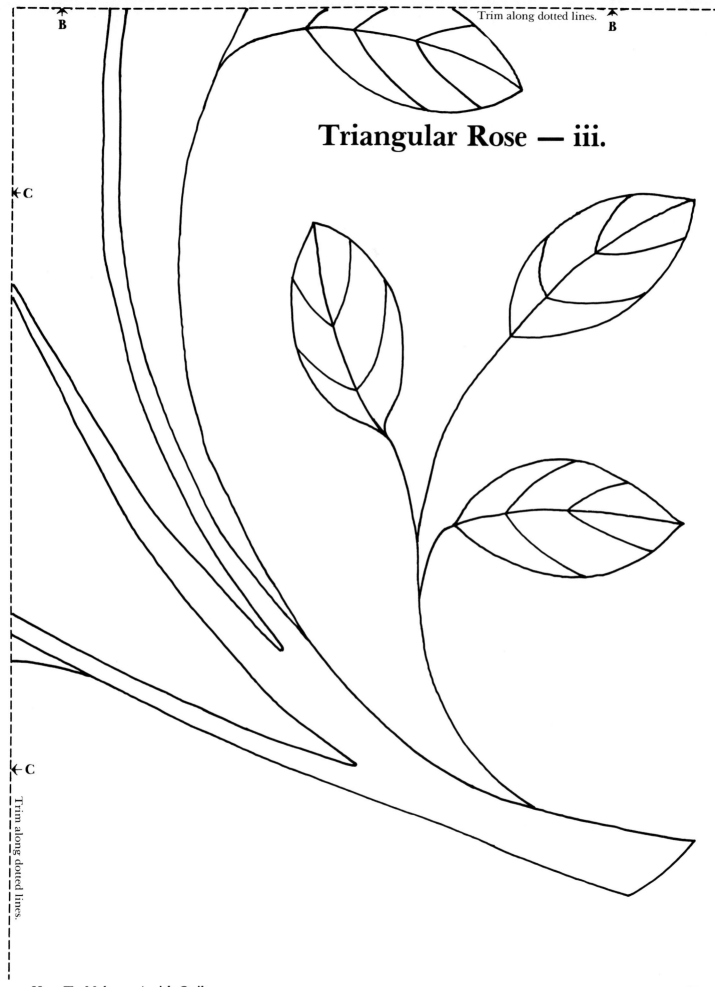

C

Triangular Rose — iii.

C

D

D

← E

C →

Triangular Rose — iv.

C →

← E

How To Make an Amish Quilt

205

Triangular Rose — v.

Ivy Leaf

E →

E →

Feather Border — i.

← A

Completed pattern motif will look like this:

To create finished template, match corresponding letters along dotted lines, and tape.

A

B →

Feather Border — ii.

B →

C

C

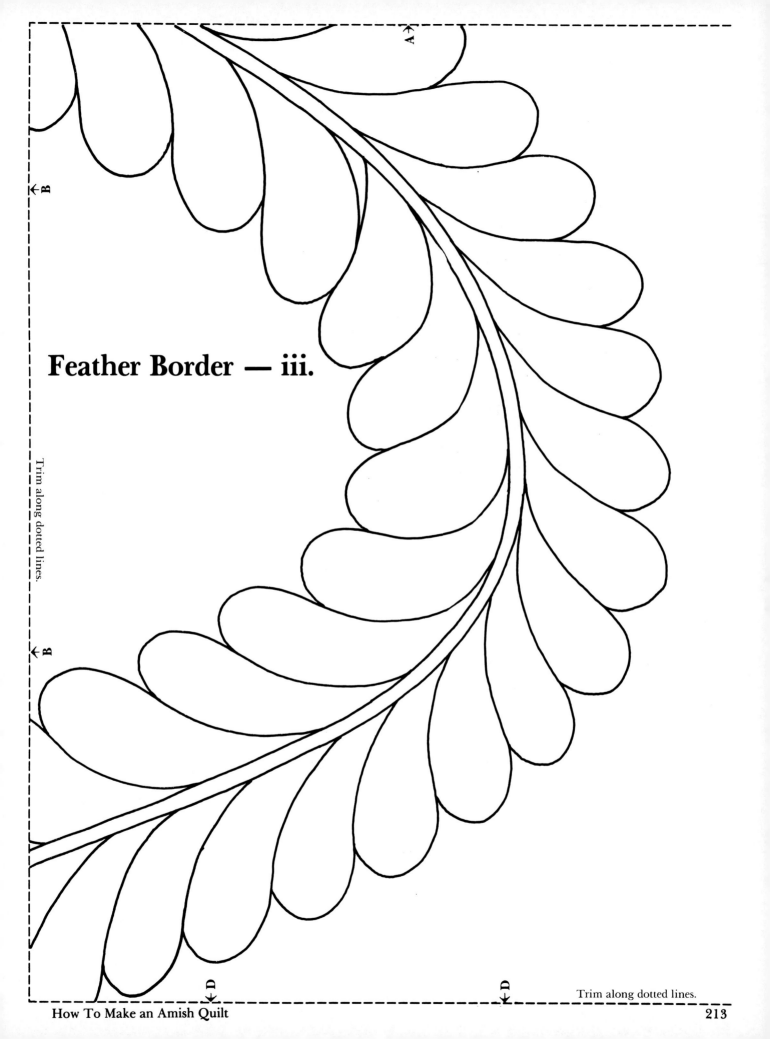

Feather Border — iii.

A

B

B

D

D

Feather Border — iv.

Trim along dotted lines.

Trim along dotted lines.

E

E

E

Feather Border — v.

E →

E →

D ↓   D ↓

Trim along dotted lines.

Grapes with Leaves

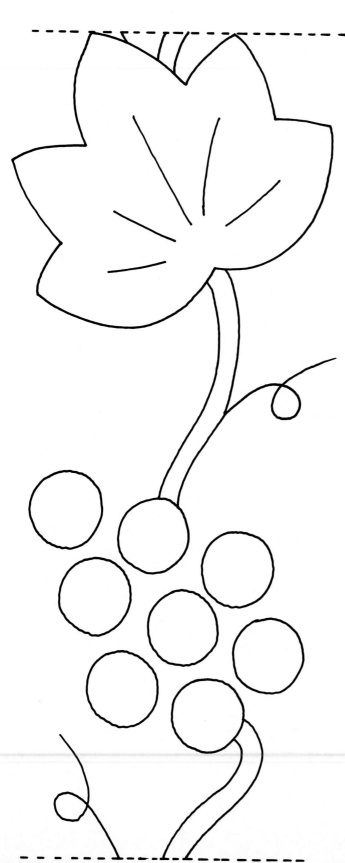

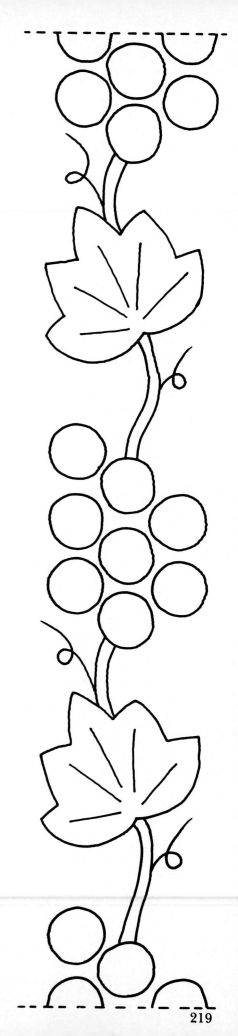

Fiddlehead Fern — i.

To create finished template, match corresponding letters
along dotted lines, and tape.

Completed pattern motif will look like this:

Trim along dotted lines.

A →

D

Trim along dotted lines.

D

Fiddlehead Fern — ii.

←A

←A

B

B

Trim along dotted lines.

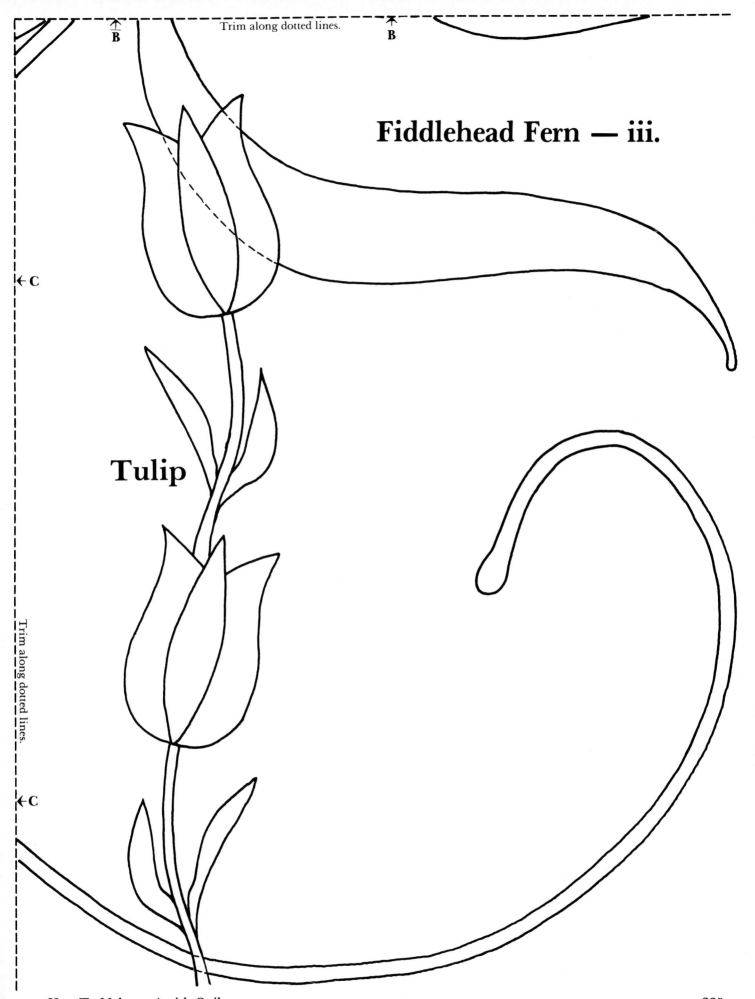

Trim along dotted lines.

Fiddlehead Fern — iii.

Tulip

Cable — iii.

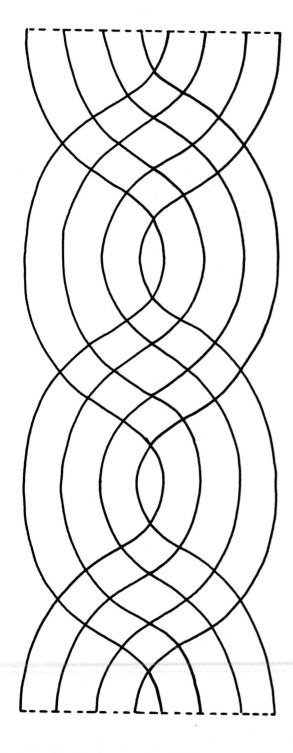

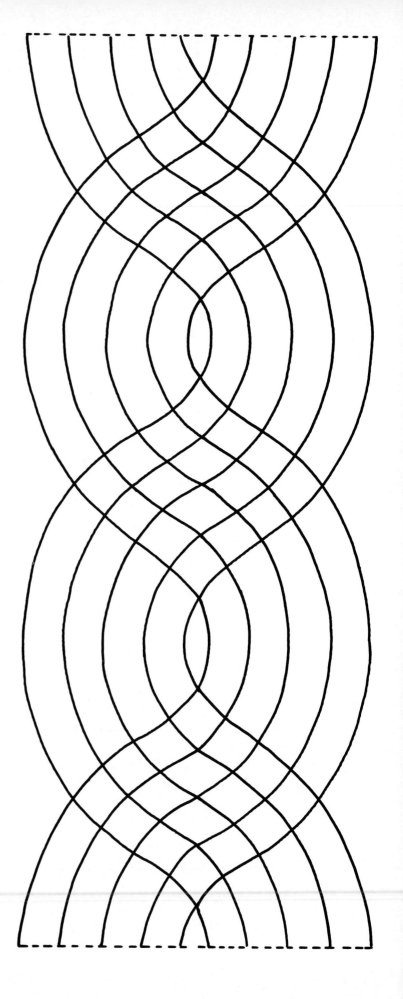

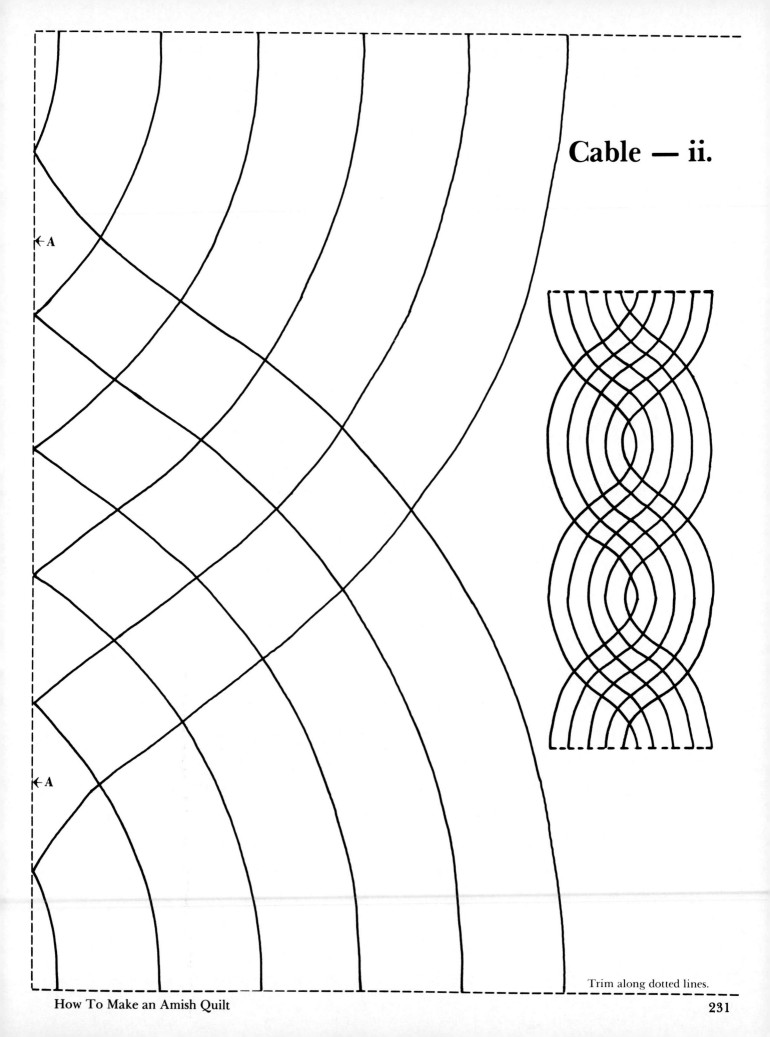

Cable — ii.

←A

←A

Trim along dotted lines.

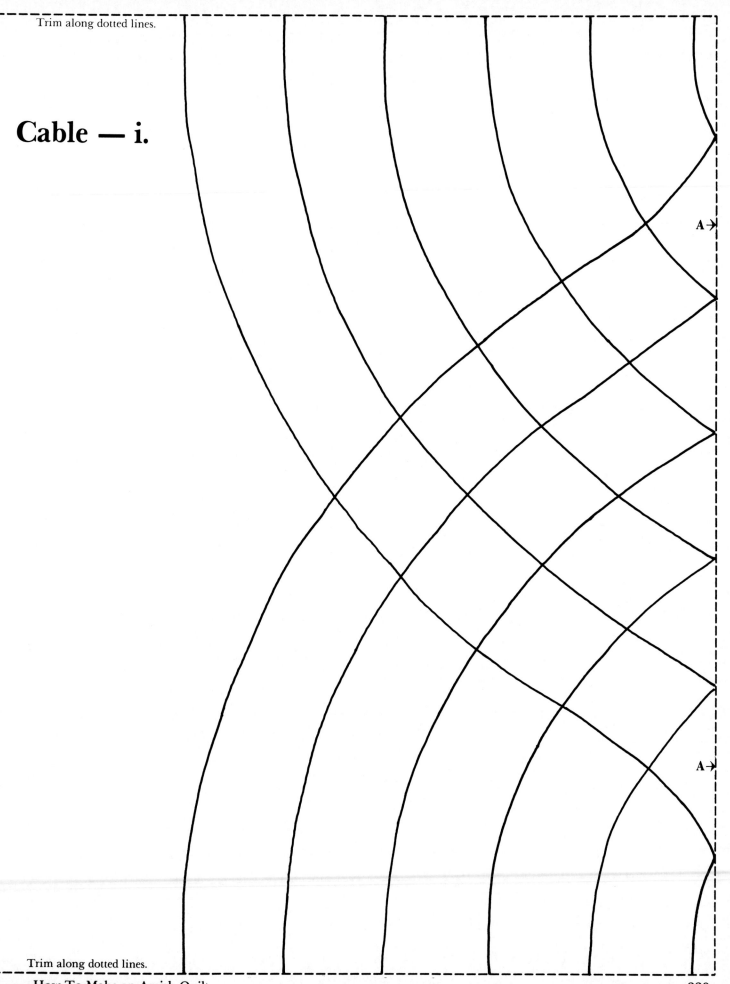

Trim along dotted lines.

Cable — i.

A →

A →

Trim along dotted lines.

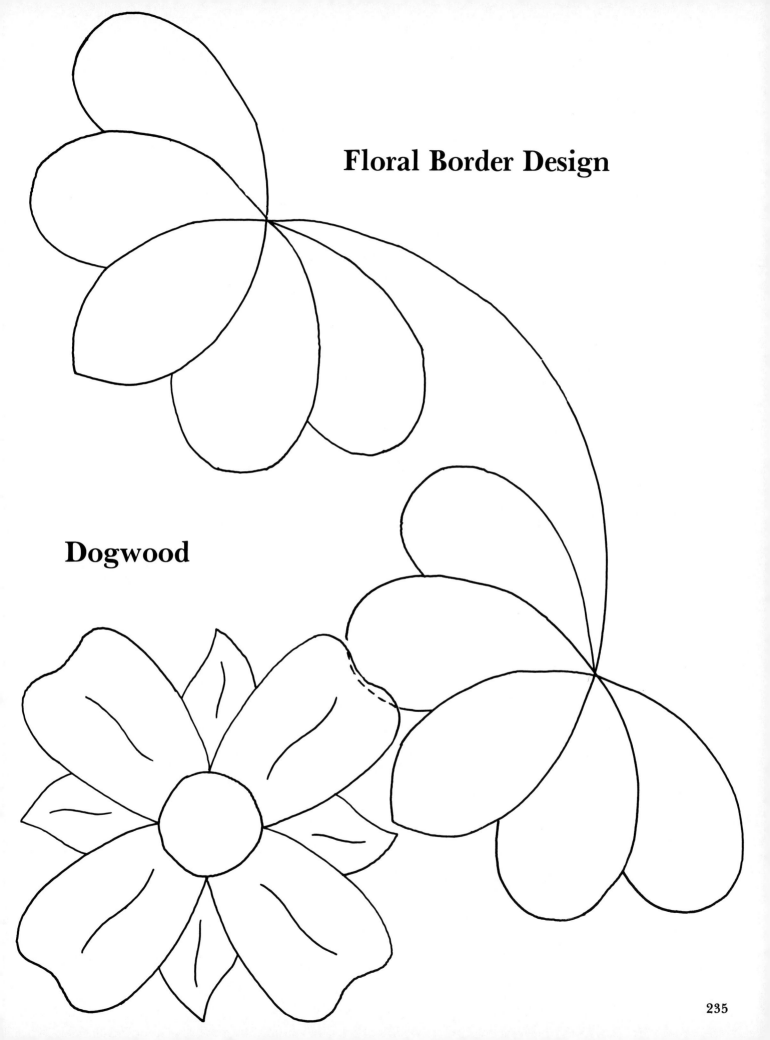

Floral Border Design

Dogwood

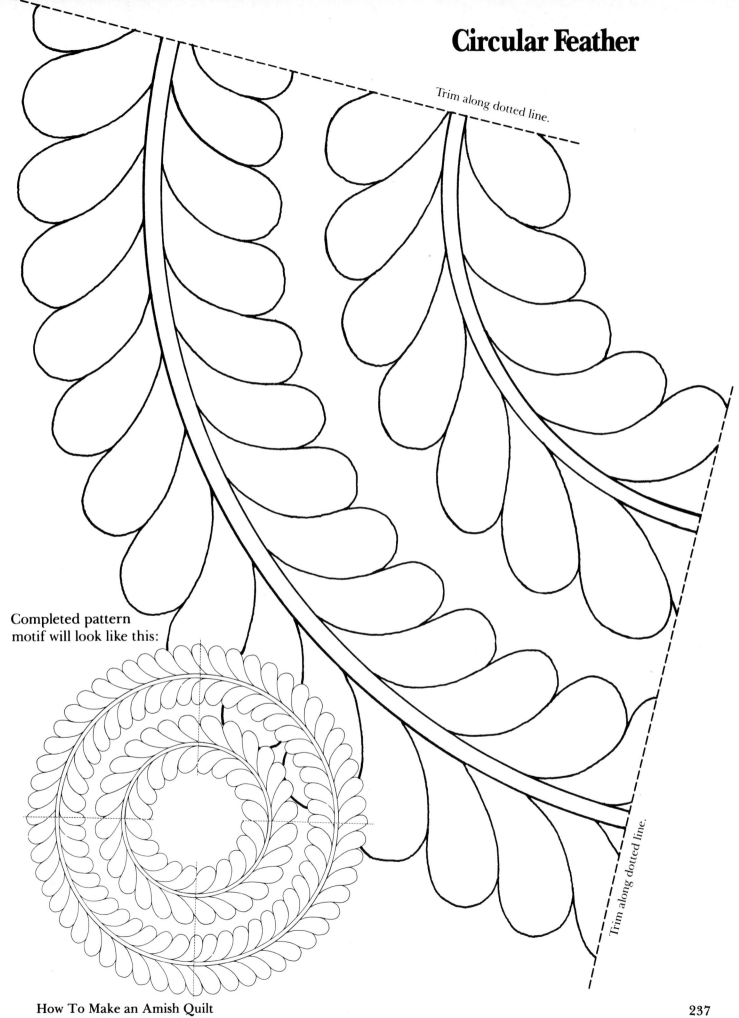

Circular Feather

Trim along dotted line.

Completed pattern
motif will look like this:

Trim along dotted line.

Triangular Rose—i.

Completed pattern motif will look like this:

To create finished template, match corresponding letters along dotted lines, and tape.

M Trim along dotted line. M

Triangular Rose—ii.

Trim along dotted line.

M

M

Floral Corner A

Feather Border—i.

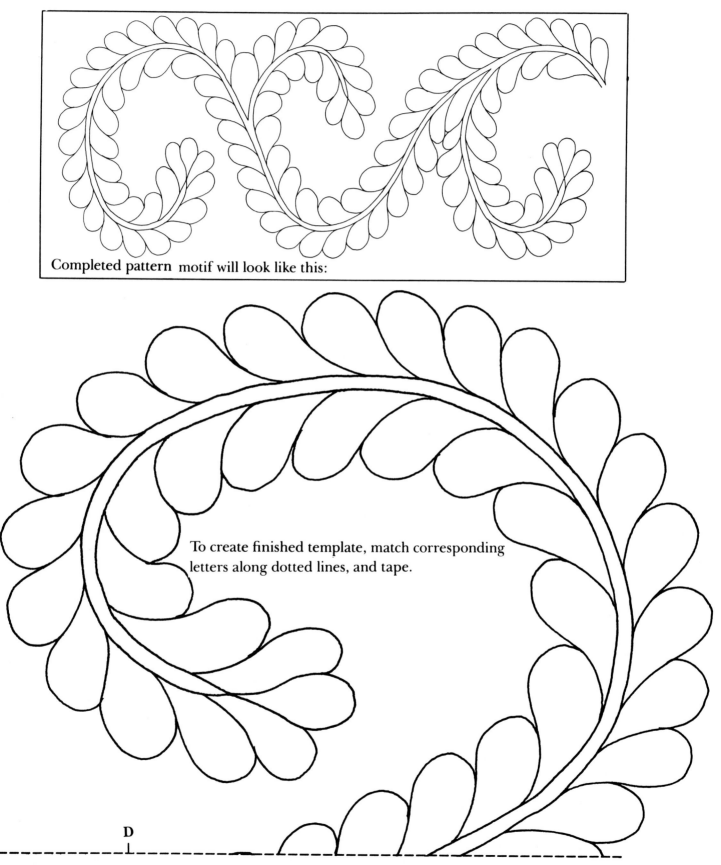

Completed pattern motif will look like this:

To create finished template, match corresponding letters along dotted lines, and tape.

D

Feather Border—ii.

Trim along dotted line.

D   D

E   E

Trim along dotted line.

Feather Border—iii.

Trim along dotted line.

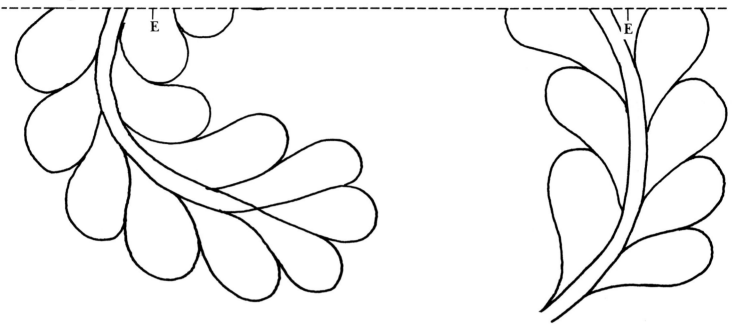

Floral Corner B

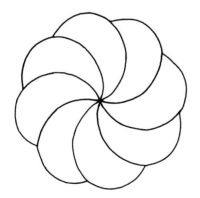

Ivy Leaf

Fiddlehead Fern—i.

Completed pattern motif will look like this:

To create finished template, match corresponding letters along dotted lines, and tape.

Trim along dotted line.

F   F

Fiddlehead Fern—ii.

Trim along dotted line.

F   F

Floral Corner C

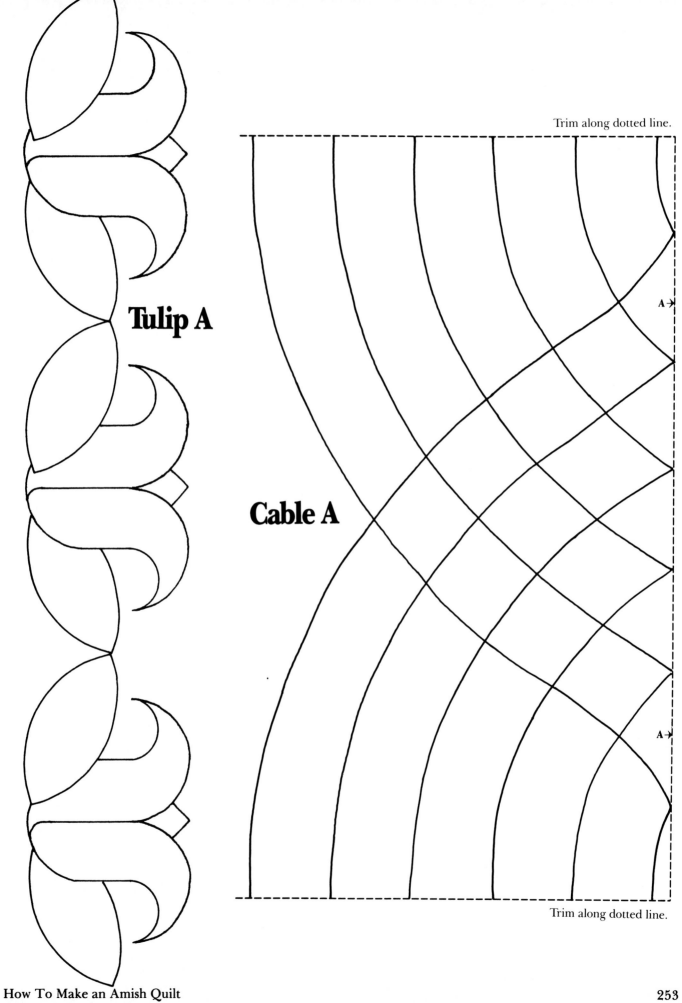

Tulip A

Cable A

Trim along dotted line.

A→

A→

Trim along dotted line.

How To Make an Amish Quilt

Trim along dotted line.

← A

← A

Cable B

Trim along dotted line.

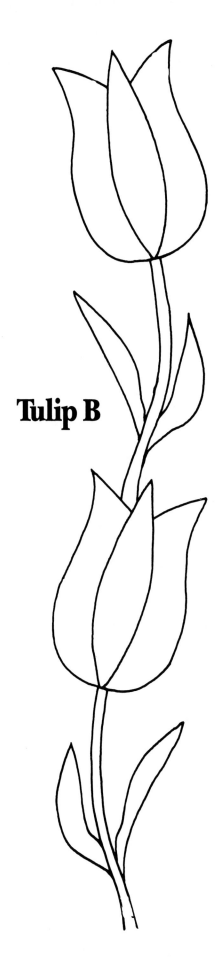

Tulip B

Grapes with Leaves

Pumpkin Seed

Floral Border Design

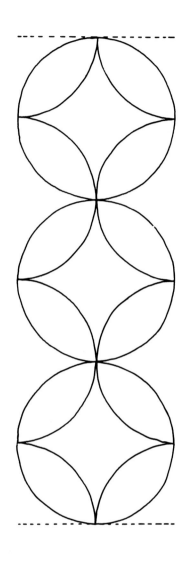

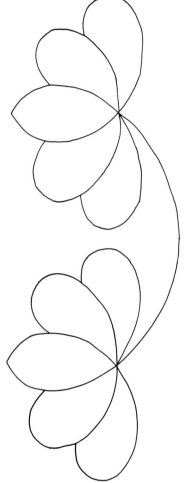

Dogwood

Fan A

Basket with Tulip—i.

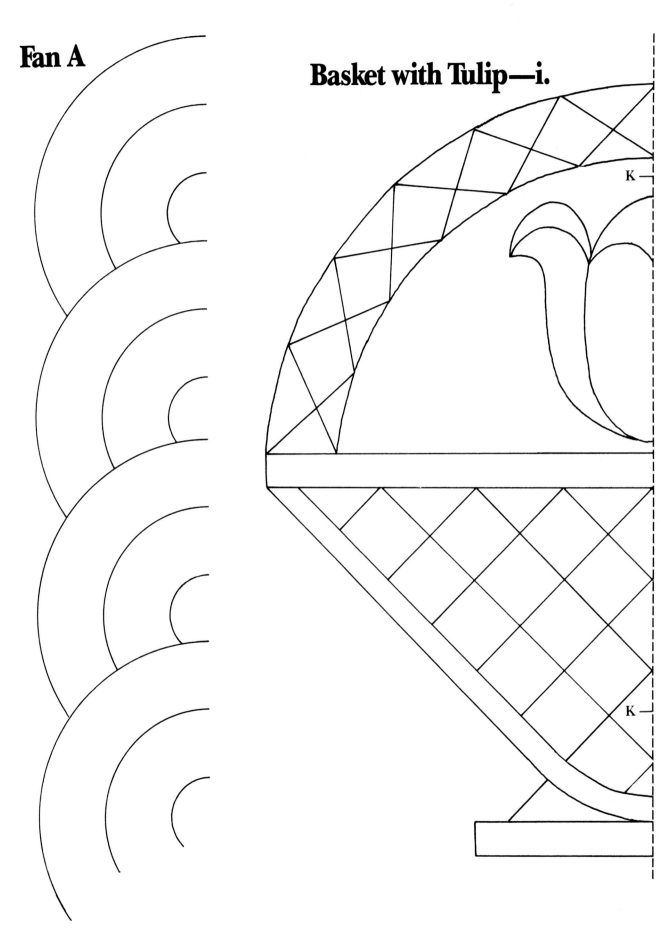

Basket with Tulip—ii.

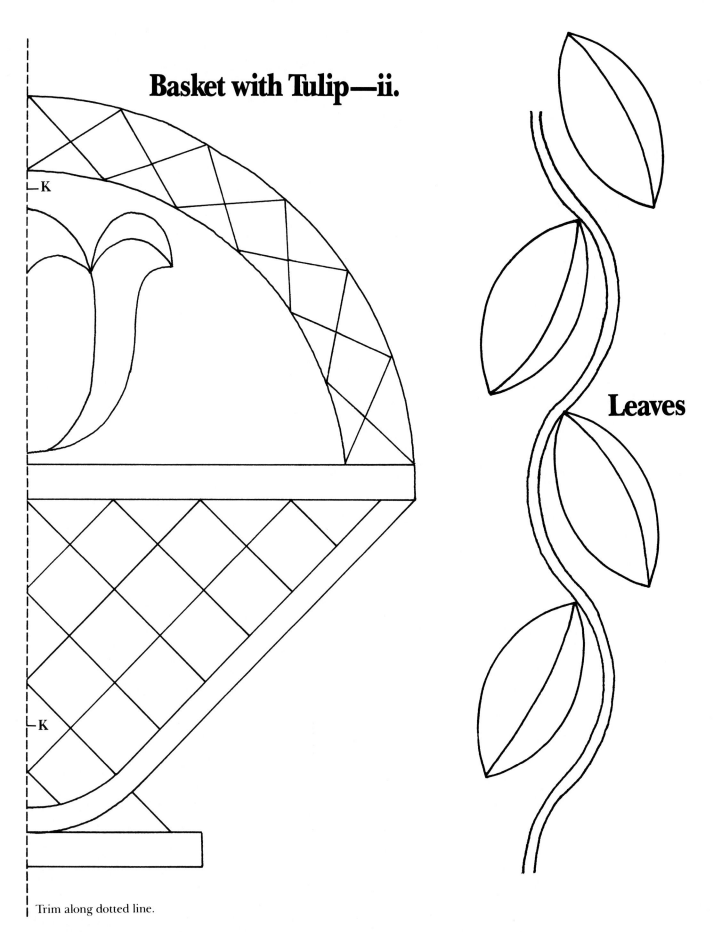

K

K

Leaves

Trim along dotted line.

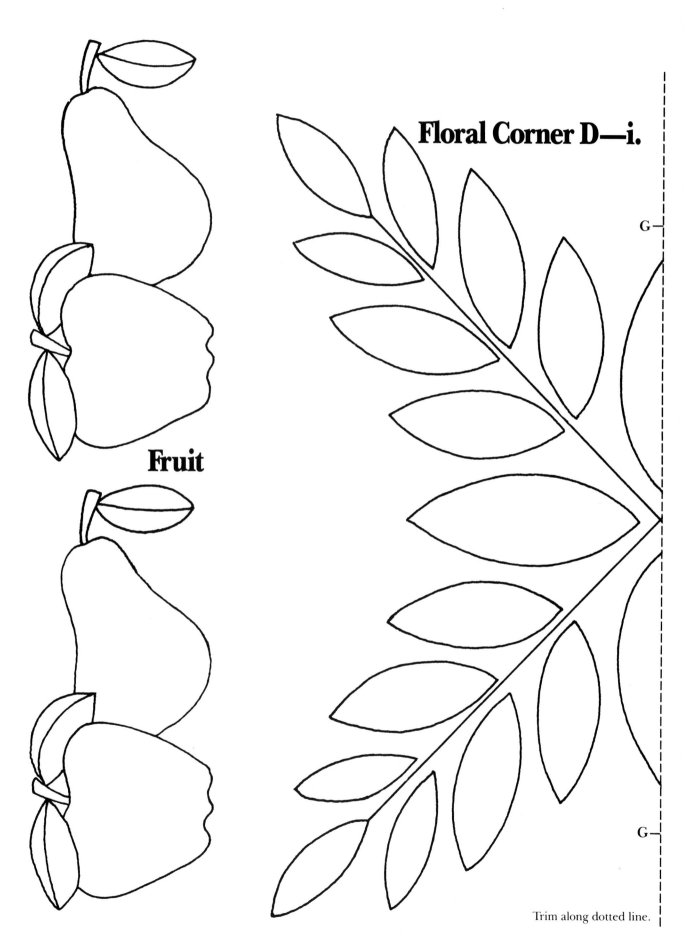

Floral Corner D—i.

Fruit

G—

G—

G—

Trim along dotted line.

Floral Corner D—ii.

Baskets

G—

G—

Trim along dotted line.

Feather Heart with Cross-Hatching

Fan B

Diamond

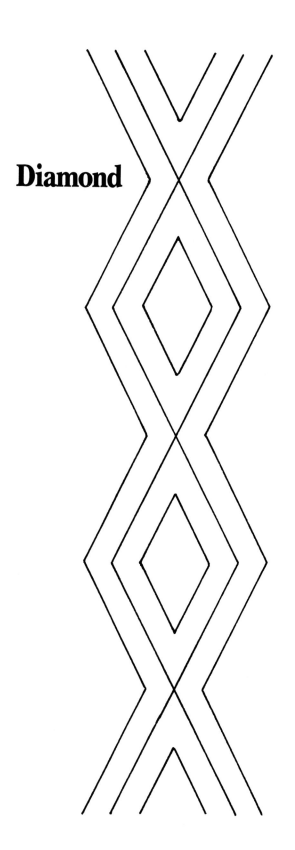

Floral Corner E

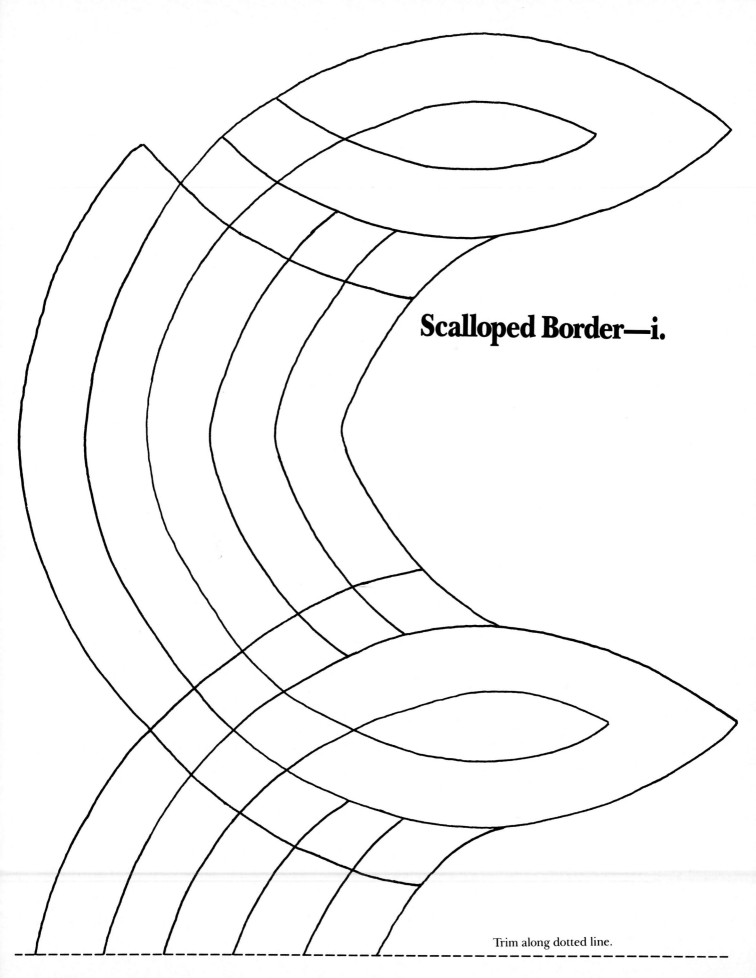

Scalloped Border—i.

Trim along dotted line.

Scalloped Border—ii.

Trim along dotted line.

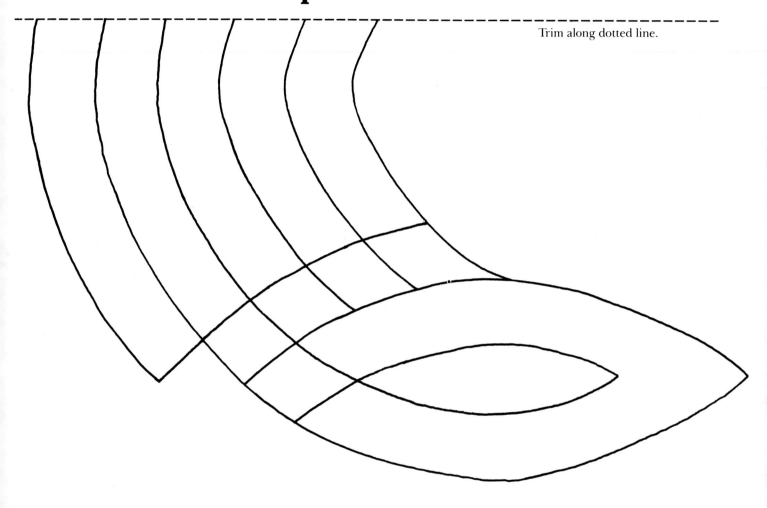

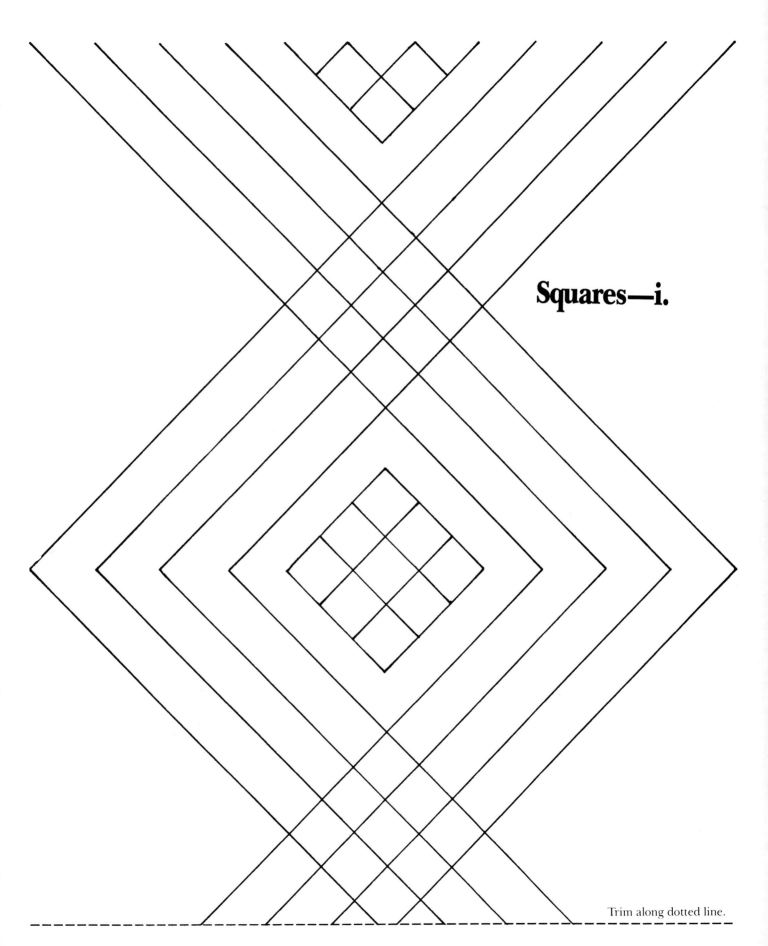

Squares—i.

Trim along dotted line.

Squares—ii.

Trim along dotted line.

Hearts

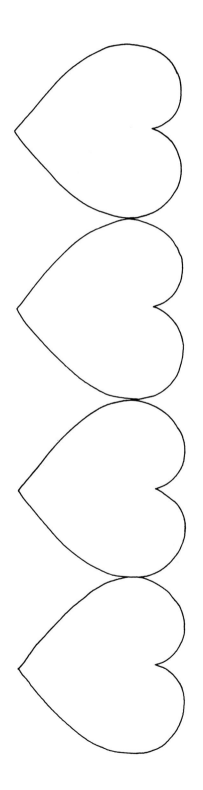

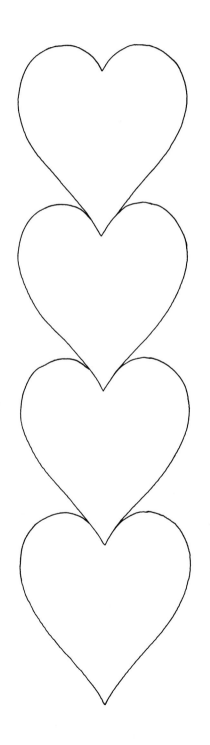

Readings and Sources

About Antique Amish Quilts

Bishop, Robert and Elizabeth Safanda. **A Gallery of Amish Quilts.** E. P. Dutton and Company, Inc., New York, New York, 1976.

Haders, Phyllis. **Sunshine and Shadow: The Amish and Their Quilts.** Universe Books, New York, New York, 1976.

Horton, Roberta. **Amish Adventure.** C & T Publishing. Lafayette, California, 1983.

Lawson, Suzy. **Amish Inspirations.** Amity Publications. Cottage Grove, Oregon, 1982.

Pottinger, David. **Quilts from the Indiana Amish.** E. P. Dutton, Inc., New York, New York, 1983.

About Other Quilts

Beyer, Jinny. **Patchwork Patterns.** EPM Publications, McLean, Virginia, 1979.

Danneman, Barbara. **Step by Step Quiltmaking.** Golden Press, Western Publishing Company, Inc., New York, New York, 1975.

Haders, Phyllis. **The Warner Collector's Guide to American Quilts.** The Main Street Press, New York, New York, 1981.

Hall, Carrie A. and Rose G. Kretsinger. **The Romance of the Patchwork Quilt in America.** Bonanza Books, New York, New York, 1935.

Hassel, Carla J. **You Can Be A Super Quilter!** Wallace-Homestead Book Company, Des Moines, Iowa, 1980.

Holstein, Jonathan. **The Pieced Quilt: An American Design Tradition.** New York Graphic Society, Boston, Massachusetts, 1973.

Houck, Carter and Myron Miller. **American Quilts and How to Make Them.** Charles Scribner's Sons, New York, New York, 1975.

Leone, Diana. **The Sampler Quilt.** Leone Publications, Santa Clara, California, 1980.

Murwin, Susan Aylsworth and Suzzy Chalfant Payne. **Quick and Easy Patchwork on the Sewing Machine.** Dover Publications, Inc., New York, New York, 1979.

Orlovsky, Patsy, and Myron Orlovsky. **Quilts in America.** McGraw Hill Book Company, New York, New York, 1974.

Pellman, Rachel T. and Joanne Ranck. **Quilts Among the Plain People.** Good Books, Intercourse, Pennsylvania, 1981.

About the Amish

Amish Cooking. Pathway Publishers, Aylmer, Ontario, 1965.

Bender, H. S. **The Anabaptist Vision.** Herald Press, Scottdale, Pennsylvania, 1967.

Braght, Thieleman J. van, Comp. **The Bloody Theatre; or, Martyrs Mirror.** Scottdale, Pennsylvania, 1951.

Budget, The. Sugarcreek, Ohio, 1890. A weekly newspaper serving the Amish and Mennonite communities.

Devoted Christian's Prayer Book. Pathway Publishing House, Aylmer, Ontario, 1967.

Family Life. Amish periodical published monthly. Pathway Publishing House, Aylmer, Ontario.

Gingerich, Orland. **The Amish of Canada.** Conrad Press. Waterloo, Ontario, 1972.

Good, Merle and Phyllis Pellman Good. **20 Most Asked Questions about the Amish and Mennonites.** Good Books, Lancaster, Pennsylvania, 1979.

Good, Phyllis Pellman and Rachel Thomas Pellman. **From Amish and Mennonite Kitchens.** Good Books, Intercourse, Pennsylvania, 1984.

Hostetler, John A. **Amish Life.** Herald Press, Scottdale, Pennsylvania, 1959.

Hostetler, John A. **Amish Society.** Johns Hopkins University Press, Baltimore, Maryland, 1963.

Keim, Albert N. **Compulsory Education and the Amish.** Beacon Press, Boston, Massachusetts, 1975.

Klaassen, Walter. **Anabaptism: Neither Catholic nor Protestant.** Conrad Press, Waterloo, Ontario, 1972.

Schreiber, William I. **Our Amish Neighbors.** University of Chicago Press, Chicago, Illinois, 1962.

Schweider, Elmer and Dorothy Schweider. **A Peculiar People: Iowa's Old Order Amish.** Iowa State University Press, Ames, Iowa, 1975.

Index

About the Authors

Rachel Pellman is manager of the People's Place Quilt Museum, featuring a permanent collection of antique Amish quilts. She is also manager of the Old Country Store in Intercourse, Pennsylvania, which features quilts, toys and crafts made by more than 300 Amish and Mennonite artisans. She and her husband, Kenneth, are authors of *The World of Amish Quilts* and *Amish Doll Quilts, Dolls, and Other Playthings.* She also has written *Amish Quilt Patterns* and *Small Amish Quilt Patterns,* and has collaborated on *The Country Bride Quilt, Quilts Among the Plain People, From Amish and Mennonite Kitchens* and 12 Pennsylvania Dutch cookbooks.

Kenneth R. Pellman is manager of The People's Place, an educational center concerned with Amish and Mennonite arts, faith and culture. Kenny graduated from Eastern Mennonite College, where he taught drama for one year. His photography appears in several books, including a National Geographic publication. He is currently working on two more manuscripts that deal with Amish and Mennonite themes.

The Pellmans live in Lancaster, Pennsylvania, with their sons, Nathaniel and Jesse.